EASY PIANO

HIGH SCHOOL MUSICAL

CONTENTS

ISBN-13: 978-1-4234-4749-8
ISBN-10: 1-4234-4749-2

Walt Disney Music Company
Wonderland Music Company, Inc.

DISTRIBUTED BY

HAL•LEONARD®
CORPORATION
7777 W. BLUEMOUND RD. P.O. BOX 13819 MILWAUKEE, WI 53213

In Australia Contact:
Hal Leonard Australia Pty. Ltd.
4 Lentara Court
Cheltenham, Victoria, 3192 Australia
Email: ausadmin@halleonard.com

Visit Hal Leonard Online at
www.halleonard.com

WHAT TIME IS IT

Words and Music by MATTHEW GERRARD
and ROBBIE NEVIL

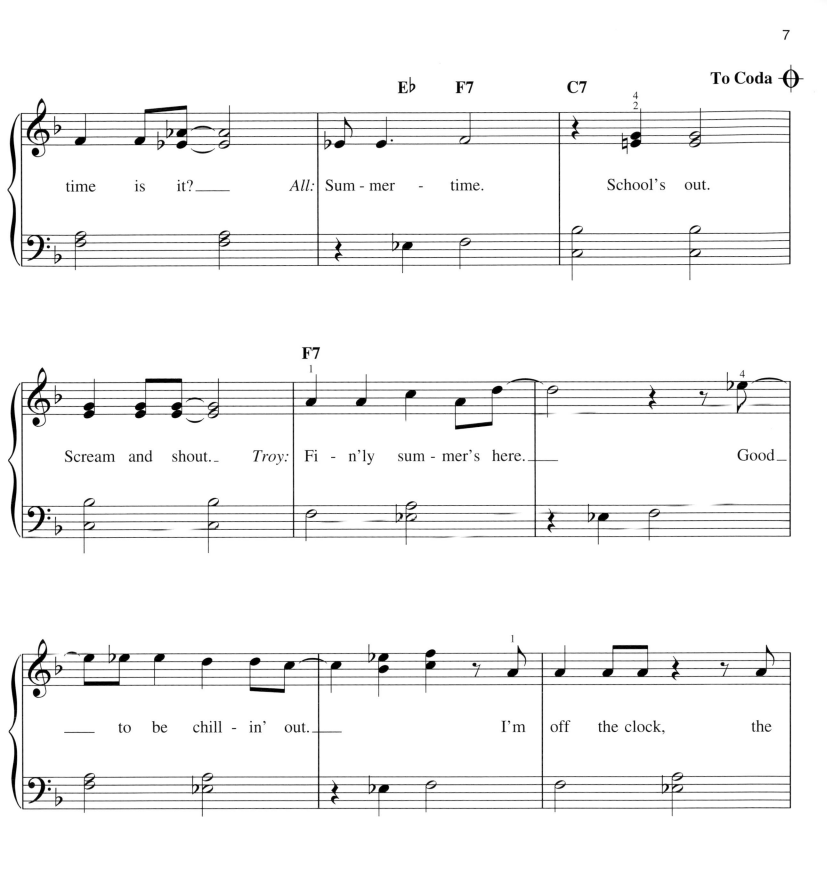

8

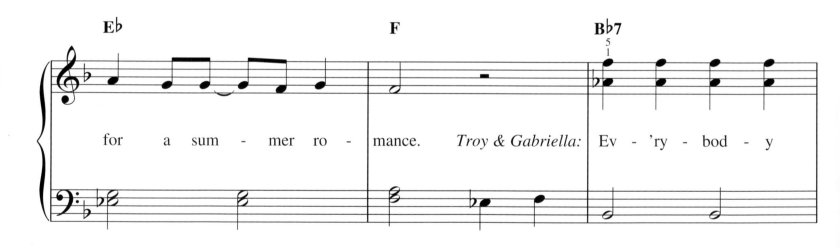

on and let me hear you say it now, right

now. *Chad:* What

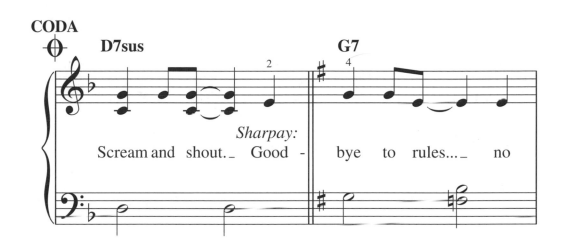

Sharpay:
Scream and shout. Good - bye to rules.... no

sum - mer school; I'm free to shop 'til I drop. *Ryan:* It's an

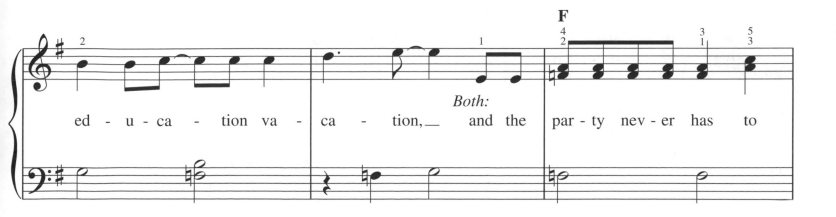

Both:
ed - u - ca - tion va - ca - tion, and the par - ty nev - er has to

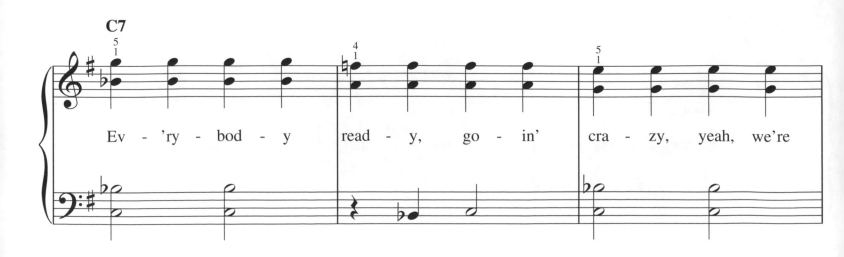

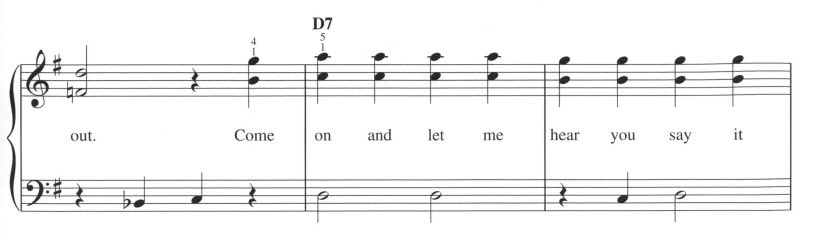

out. Come on and let me hear you say it

now, right now. *Chad:* What time is it?____

All: Sum-mer - time. It's our va - ca - tion. What

time is it?____ *All:* Par - ty time. That's right,

F   **F#**   **G7**   **F**   **G7**

Chad: *All:*

say   it   loud.__   What   time   is   it?___   The   time   of   our   lives.

F#

An - ti - ci - pa - tion.   What   time   is   it?___

Chad:

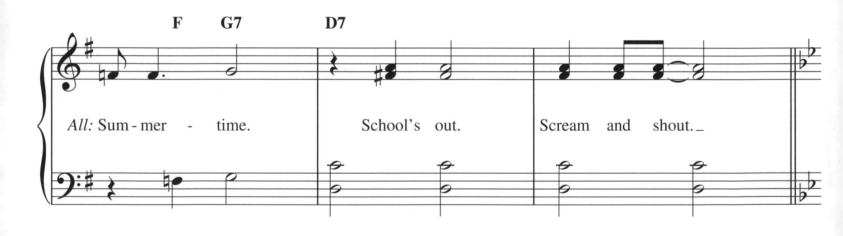

F   **G7**   **D7**

All: Sum - mer - time.   School's   out.   Scream   and   shout.__

E♭   **B♭**

Troy & Gabriella: No   more   wak - in'   up   at   six   a. -   m.,___

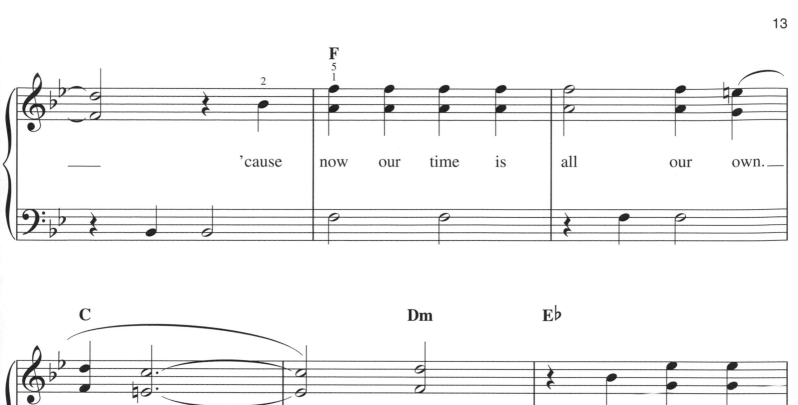

'cause now our time is all our own.

Sharpay & Ryan:
E - nough al -

read - y, we're wait - ing, come on, let's

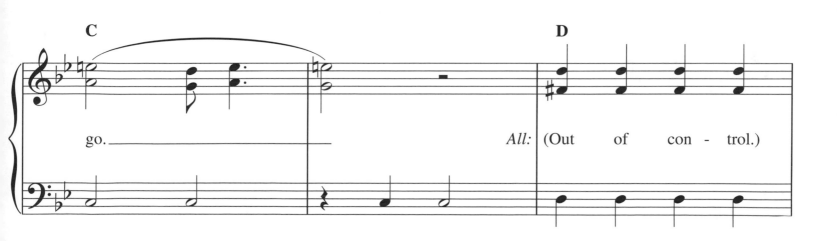

go. *All:* (Out of con - trol.)

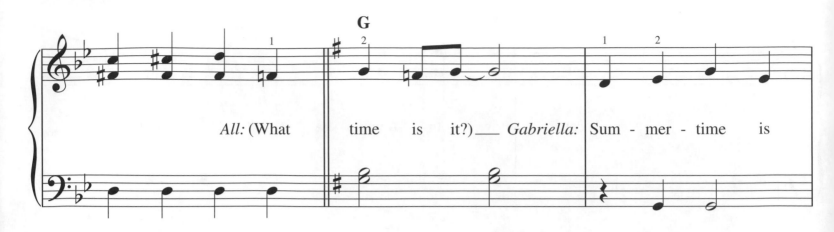

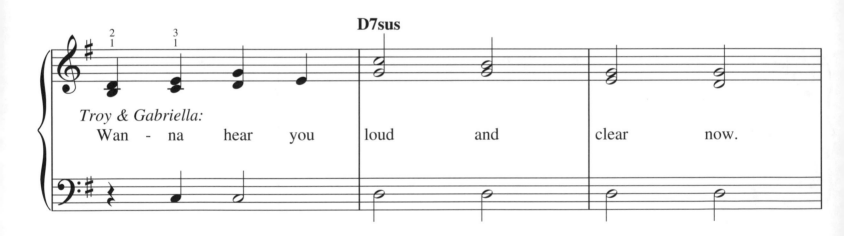

want to. (It's our time.) Now we can do what-

ev - er we wan - na do. (What time is it?)

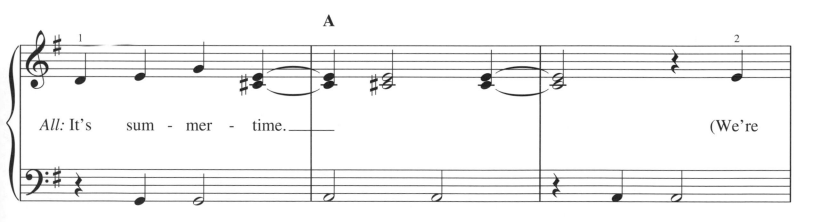

All: It's sum - mer - time. (We're

lov - in' it.) Come on and say it a - gain

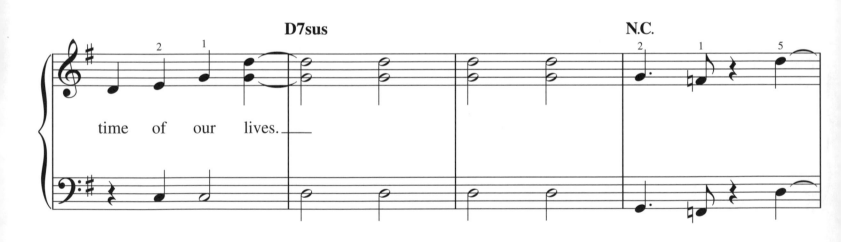

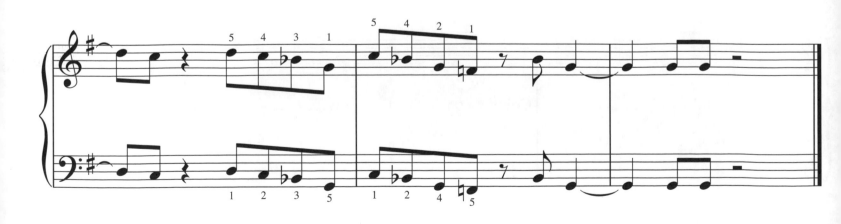

FABULOUS

Words and Music by DAVID LAWRENCE
and FAYE GREENBERG

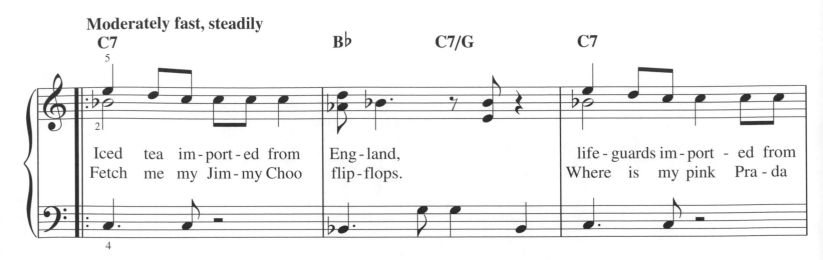

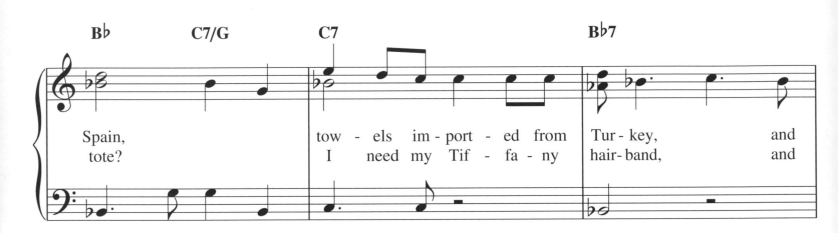

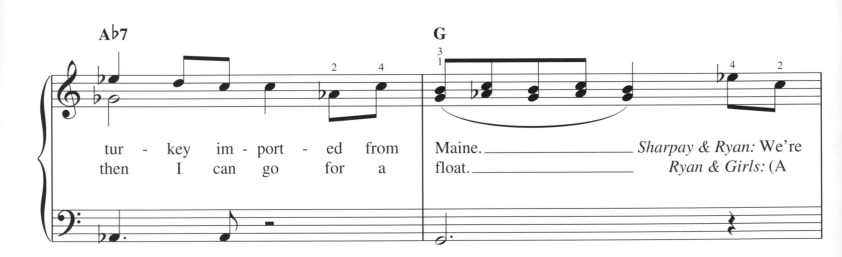

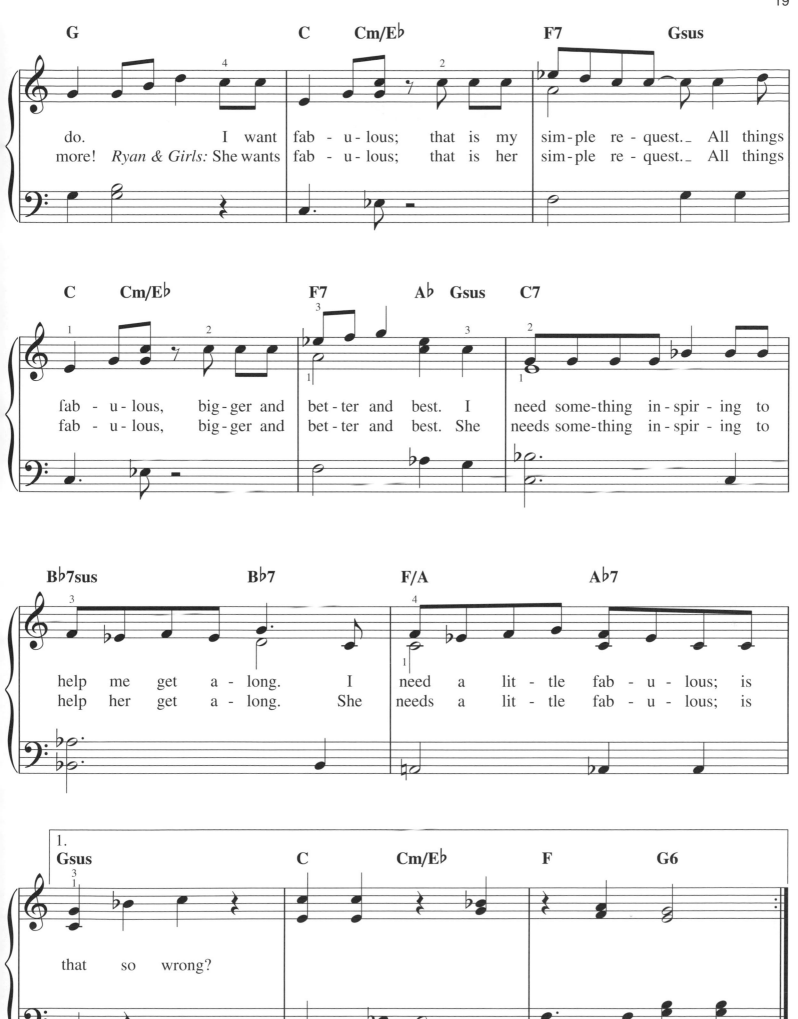

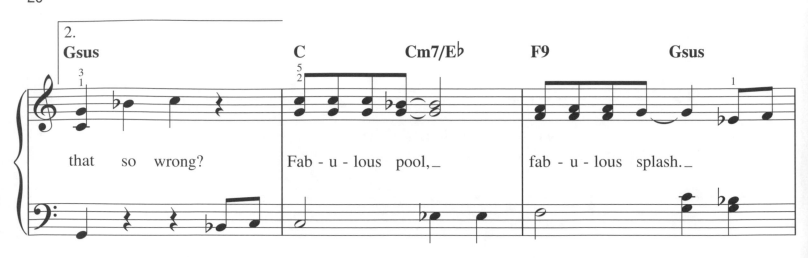

2.
Gsus   **C**   **Cm7/E♭**   **F9**   **Gsus**

that so wrong? Fab - u - lous pool, _ fab - u - lous splash. _

C   **Cm7/E♭**   **F9**   **A♭** **G7sus**   **C**   **Cm/E♭**

Fab - u - lous par - ties, e - ven fab - u - lous trash. Fab - u - lous fash - ion, fab -

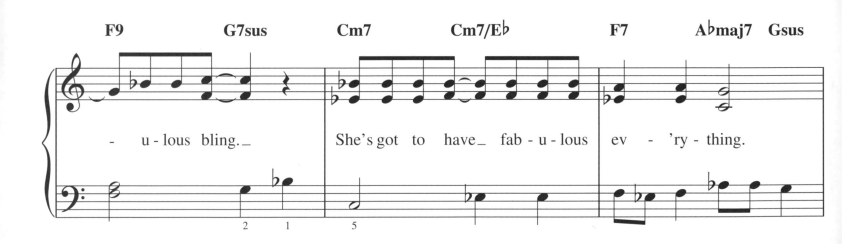

F9   **G7sus**   **Cm7**   **Cm7/E♭**   **F7**   **A♭maj7** **Gsus**

- u - lous bling. _ She's got to have _ fab - u - lous ev - 'ry - thing.

A♭7   **F♯dim**   **G5**

Ryan & Sharpay:
Noth - ing to ____ dis - cuss; ev - 'ry - thing's got to be

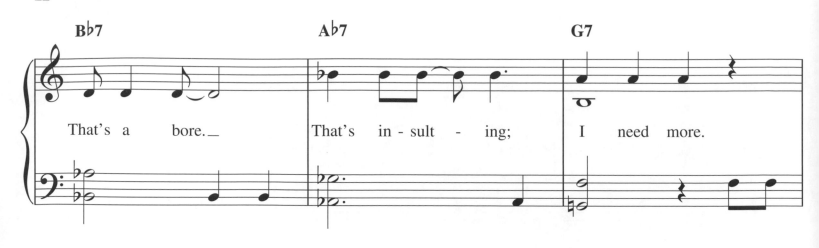

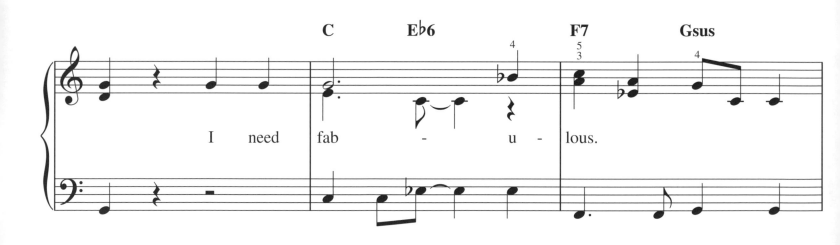

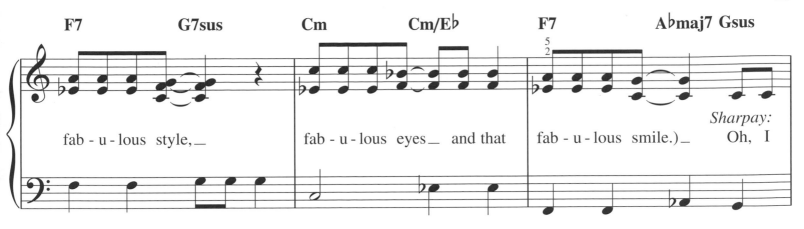

F7   G7sus   Cm   Cm/E♭   F7   A♭maj7 Gsus

fab - u - lous style,__ fab - u - lous eyes__ and that fab - u - lous smile.)__ *Sharpay:* Oh, I

C5   B♭   Am7   A♭

like what I see,__ I like it a lot.__ *Girls:* Is this ab - so - lute - ly fab - u - lous?

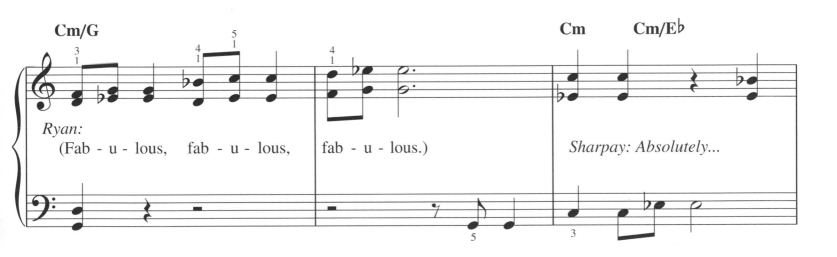

Cm/G   Cm   Cm/E♭

Ryan: (Fab - u - lous, fab - u - lous, fab - u - lous.) *Sharpay:* Absolutely...

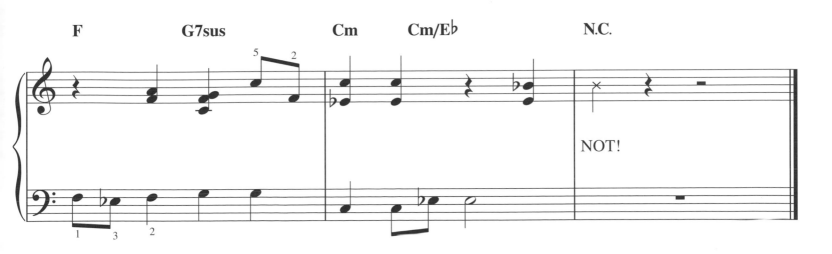

F   G7sus   Cm   Cm/E♭   N.C.

NOT!

WORK THIS OUT

Words and Music by RANDY PETERSEN
and KEVIN QUINN

Moderately fast

Chad: How did we get from the top of the world___ to the bot-tom of the heap?___

___ *Taylor:* I don't re-call___ you men-tion-in'___ the

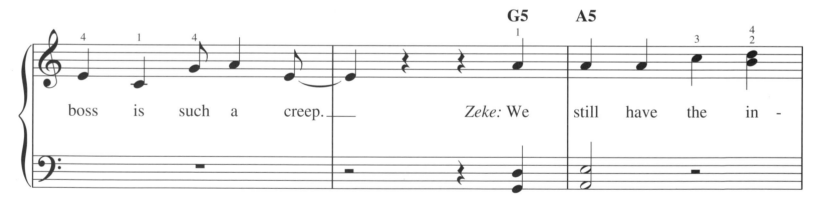

boss is such a creep.___ *Zeke:* We still have the in-

gre-di-ents___ to make this sum-mer sweet.___ *Martha:* Well,

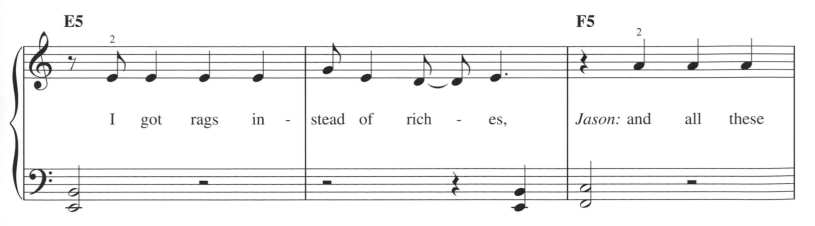

E5   **F5**

I got rags in - stead of rich - es, *Jason:* and all these

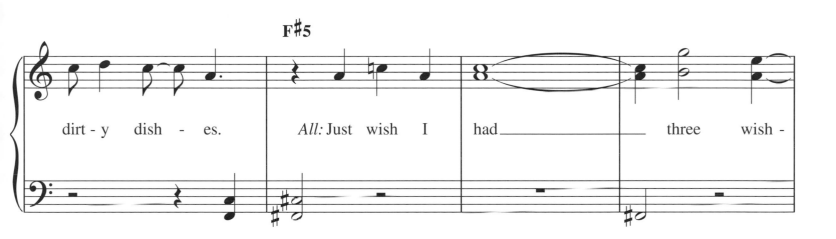

F#5

dirt - y dish - es. *All:* Just wish I had three wish -

N.C.   **Am**

- es. *Gabriella:* *Okay, guys, break it up.* *Troy:* We've got to work,

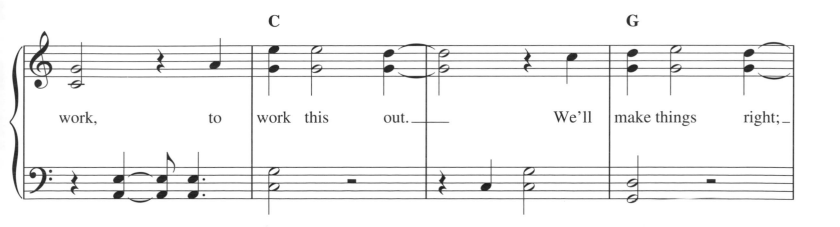

C   **G**

work, to work this out. We'll make things right;

the sun____ will shine.____ If we work,

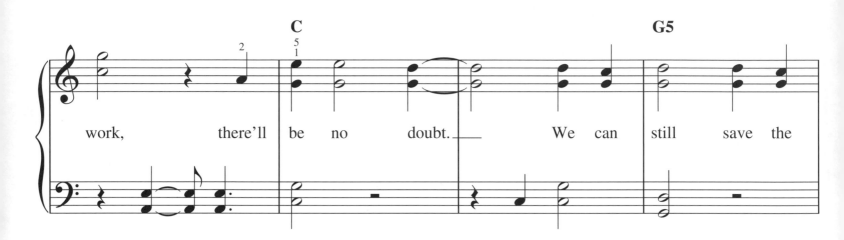

work, there'll be no doubt.____ We can still save the

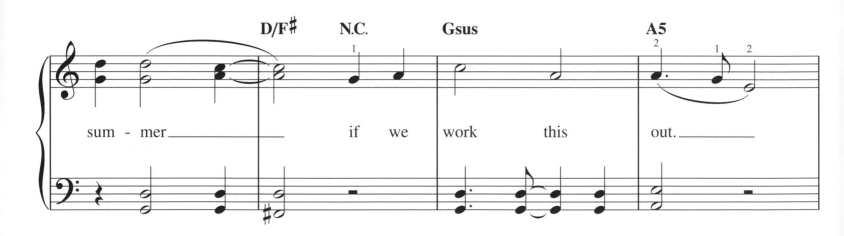

sum - mer____ if we work this out.____

Chad: Dude, what have you gotten us into?

Troy: Come on, we can totally turn this thing around. Chad: I'd rath - er face a

sev - en foot-er straight up in the post.__ Taylor: That sure beats

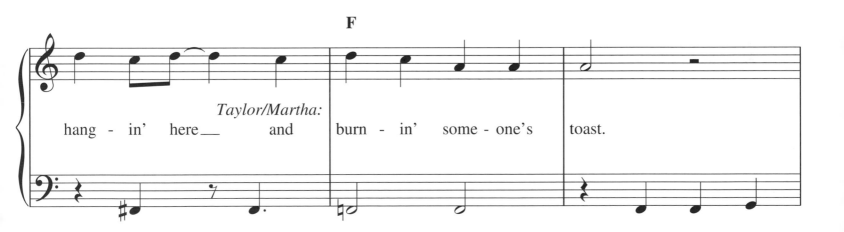

hang - in' here__ and burn - in' some - one's toast.

Jason: I need - ed Ben - ja - mins,__ but this ain't worth the stress.__

F#m7b5

Kelsi: May - be there's a bet - ter way___ to

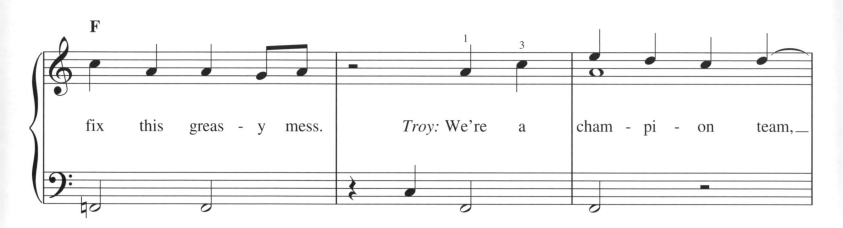

F

fix this greas - y mess. *Troy:* We're a cham - pi - on team,___

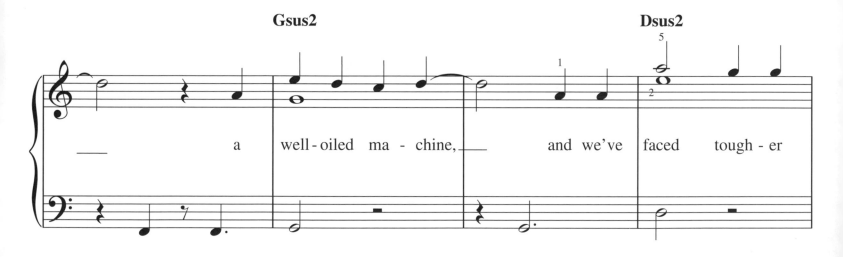

Gsus2   **Dsus2**

___ a well - oiled ma - chine,___ and we've faced tough - er

F

prob - lems than this.___ I know it's a grind,___

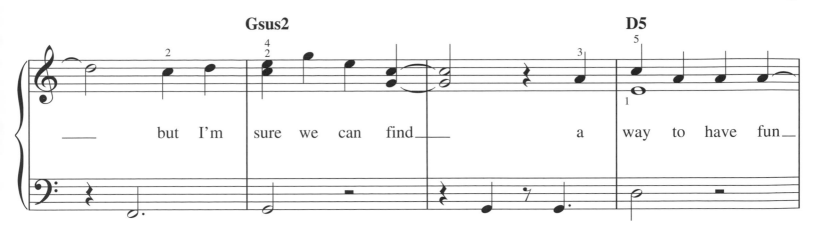

_but I'm sure we can find___ a way to have fun__

___ while we get this job done.___ We've got to work,

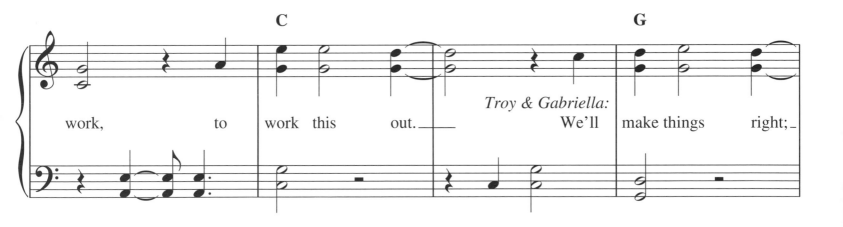

work, to work this out.___ _Troy & Gabriella:_ We'll make things right;_

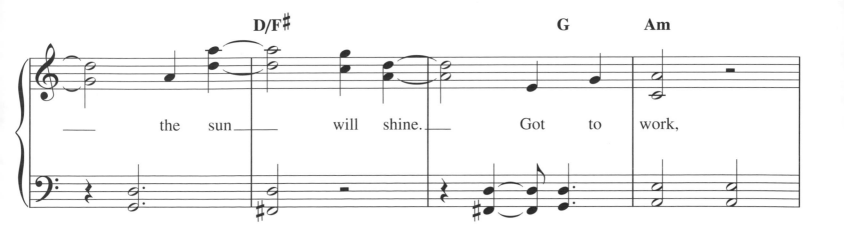

___ the sun___ will shine.___ Got to work,

work, there'll be no doubt. *T/G/Kelsi/Zeke:* If we all come to-

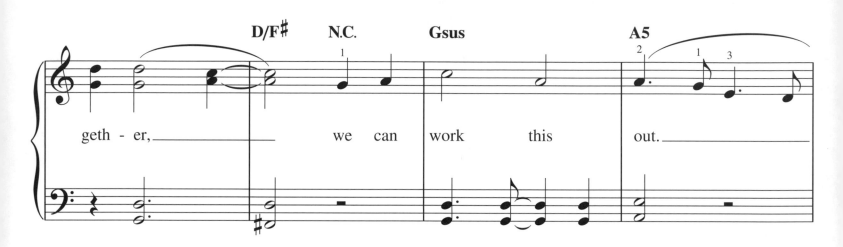

geth - er, we can work this out.

Troy: Let's work it.

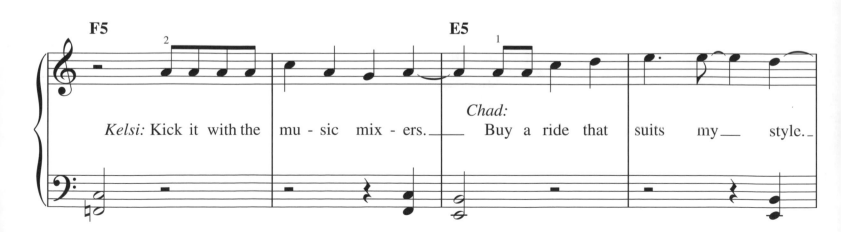

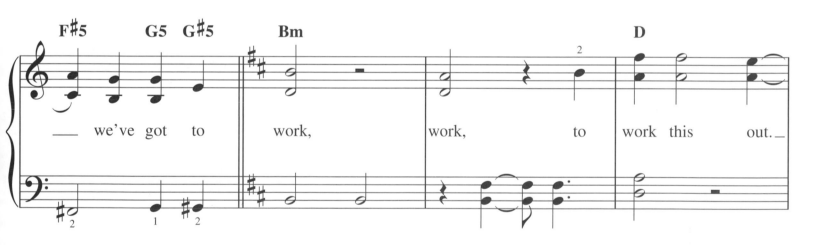

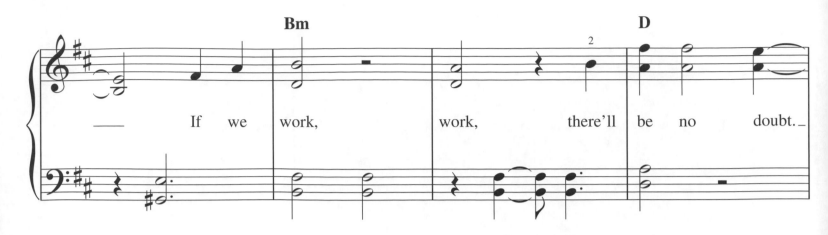

If we work, work, there'll be no doubt.

We can still save the sum - mer if we

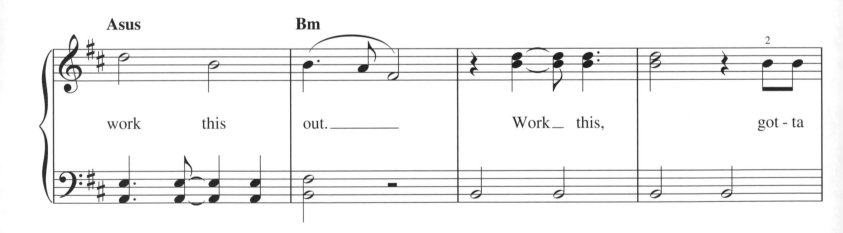

work this out. Work this, got - ta

work this. We can work this out.

EVERYDAY

Words and Music by
JAMIE HOUSTON

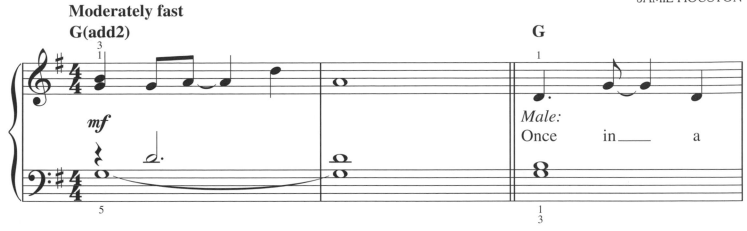

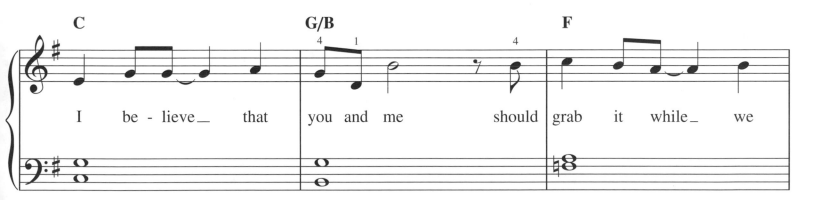

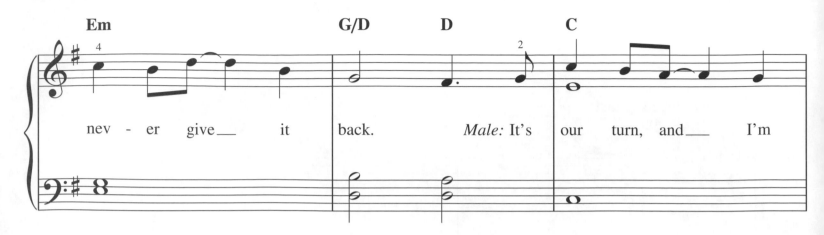

nev - er give___ it back. *Male:* It's our turn, and___ I'm

lov - in' where we're at, *Both:* be -

cause this mo - ment's real - ly all___ we have.___

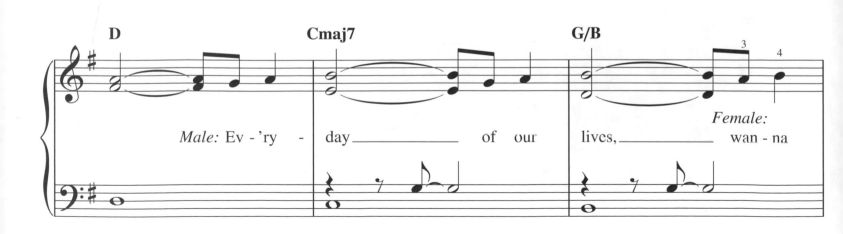

Male: Ev - 'ry - day___ of our lives,___ wan - na

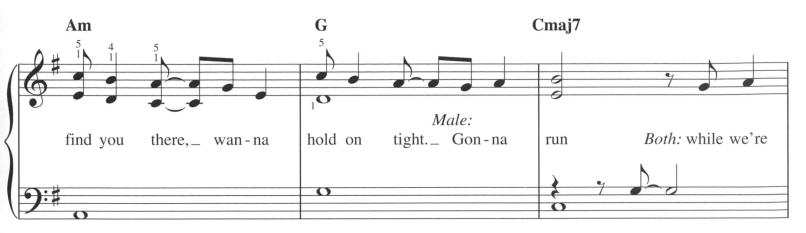

find you there,__ wan-na hold on tight.__ Gon-na run *Both:* while we're

young, and keep the faith. *Male:* Ev-'ry-

day_____ *Both:* from right now,_____ gon-na use our voic - es and

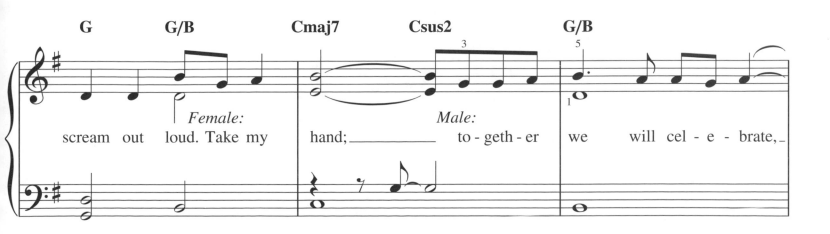

scream out loud. Take my *Female:* hand;_____ *Male:* to-geth-er we will cel-e-brate,__

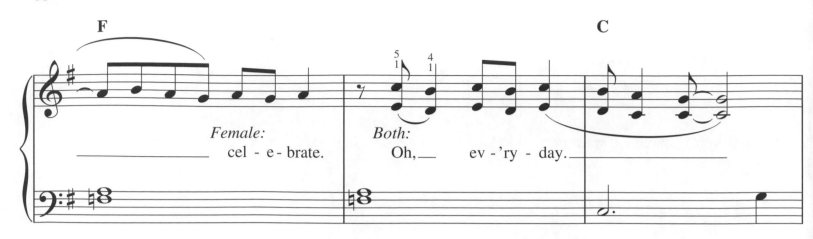

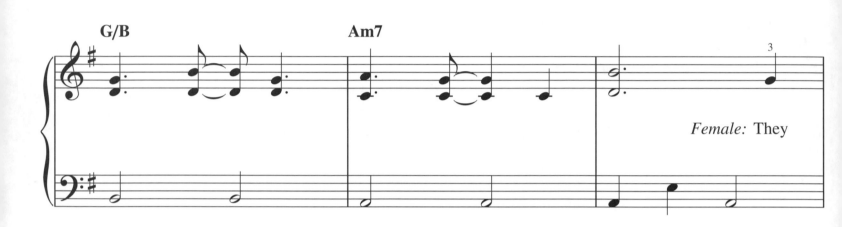

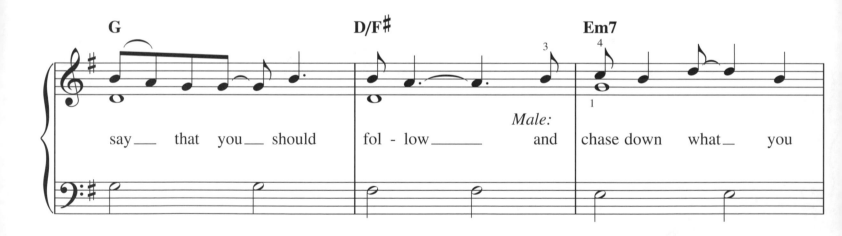

does it real - ly mean? *Female:* No mat - ter where we're

go - ing,_____ *Male:* it starts from where we are. *Female:* There's

Both:
more to life__ when we lis - ten to___ our hearts._____

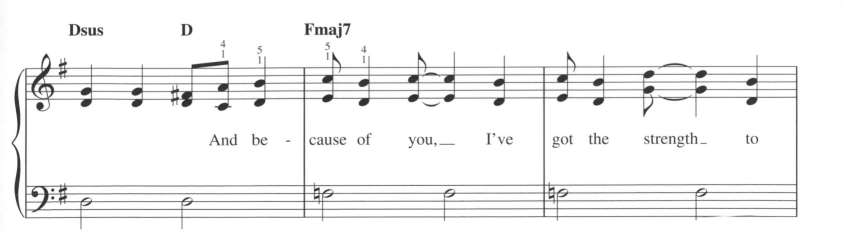

And be - cause of you,__ I've got the strength__ to

day___ *Male:* from right now,_____ gon - na use our voic - es and

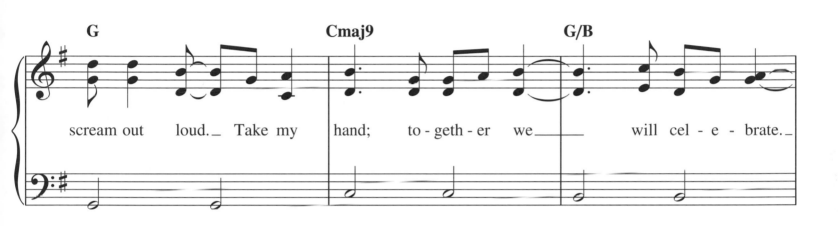

scream out loud._ Take my hand; to - geth - er we___ will cel - e - brate._

___ *Male:* We're tak - ing it back,_ we're do - ing

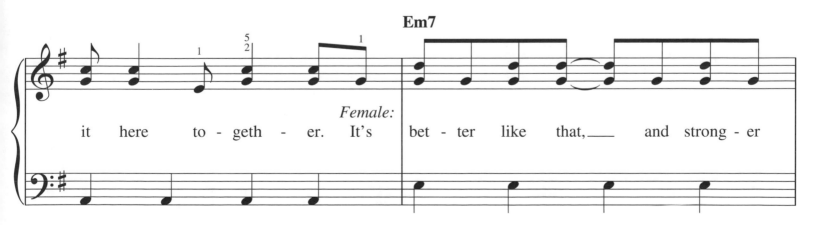

it here to - geth - er. *Female:* It's bet - ter like that,___ and strong - er

42

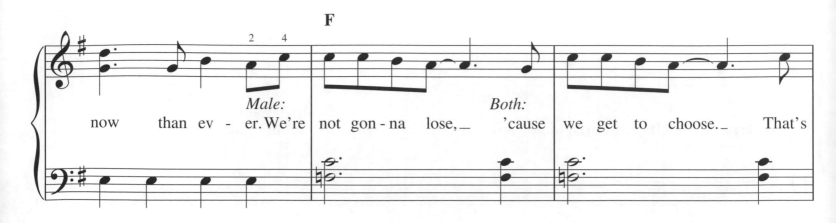

now than ev - er. We're not gon - na lose,__ 'cause we get to choose.__ That's

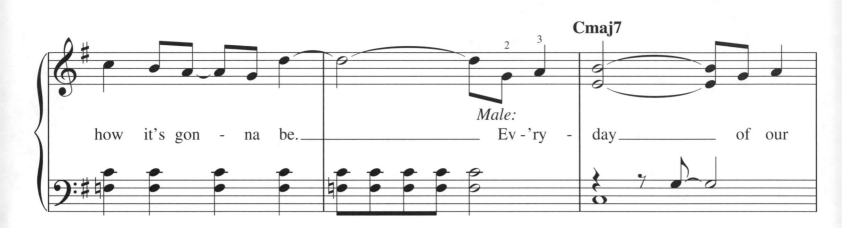

how it's gon - na be._____ Ev -'ry - day_____ of our

lives,_____ wan - na find you there,__ wan - na hold on tight.__ Gon - na

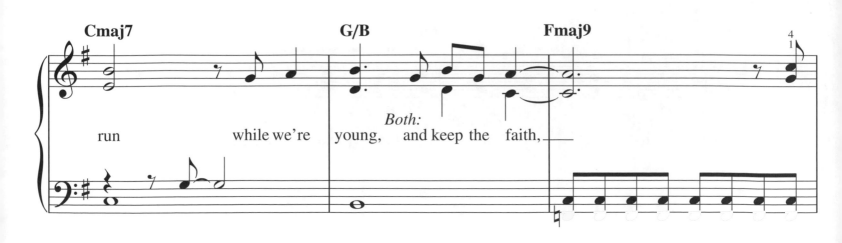

run while we're young, and keep the faith,__

keep the | faith. | *Choir:* Ev-'ry -

Cmaj7 | **G/B** | **Am**

day _____ of our | lives, _____ wan-na | find you there, _ wan-na

G | **Cmaj7** | **G/B**

hold on tight._ Gon-na | run _____ while we're | young, and keep the faith._

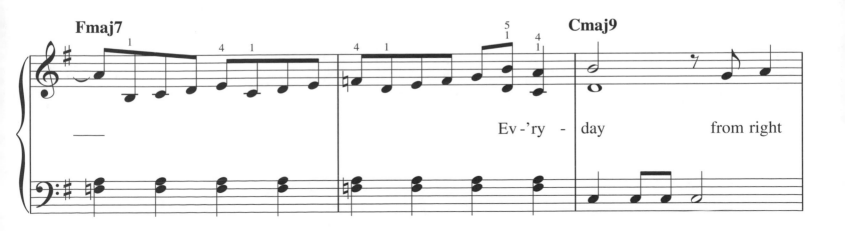

Fmaj7 | | **Cmaj9**

_____ | Ev-'ry-day | from right

44

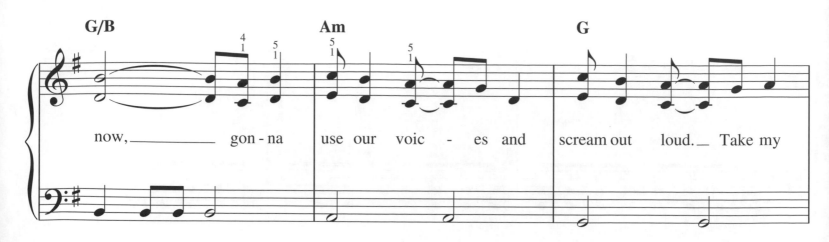

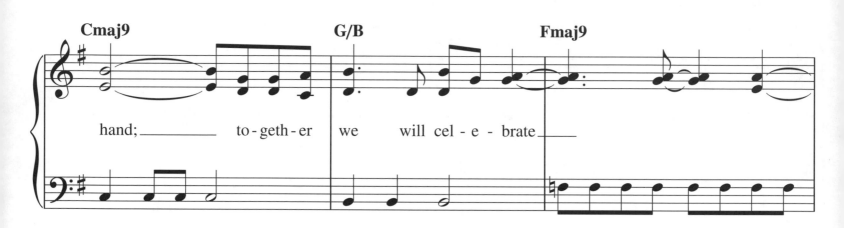

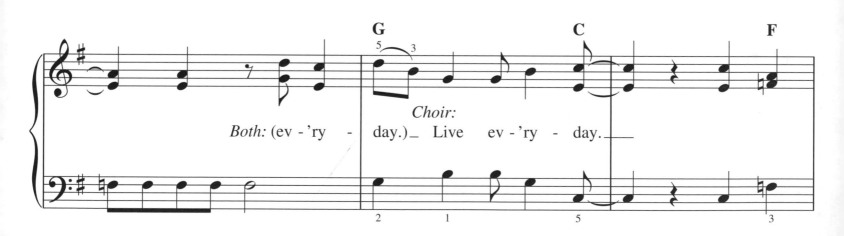

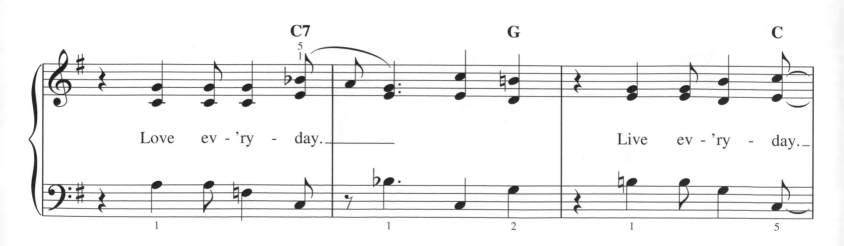

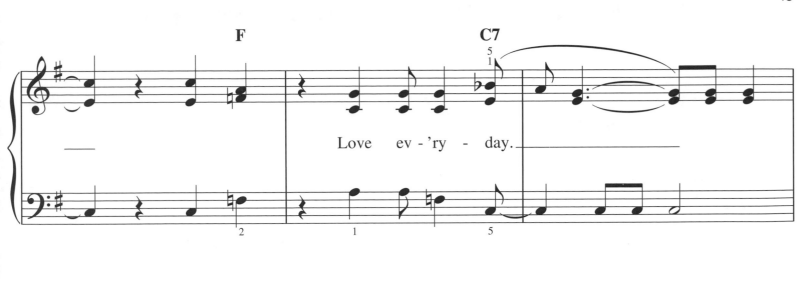

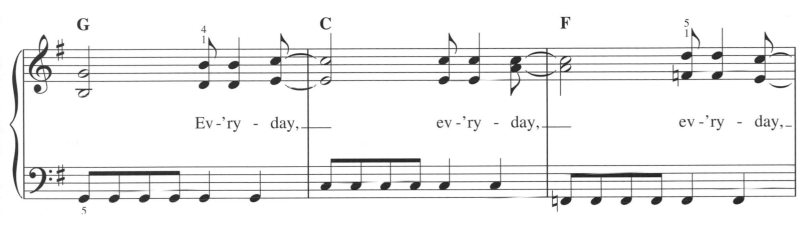

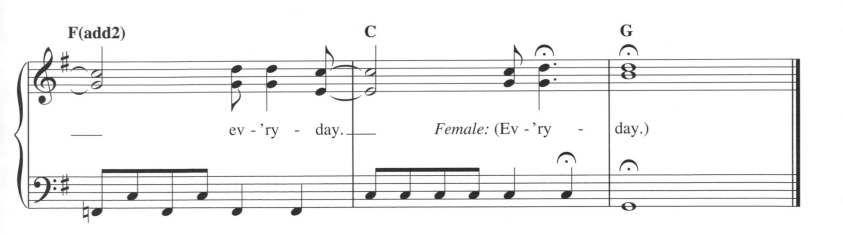

YOU ARE THE MUSIC IN ME

Words and Music by
JAMIE HOUSTON

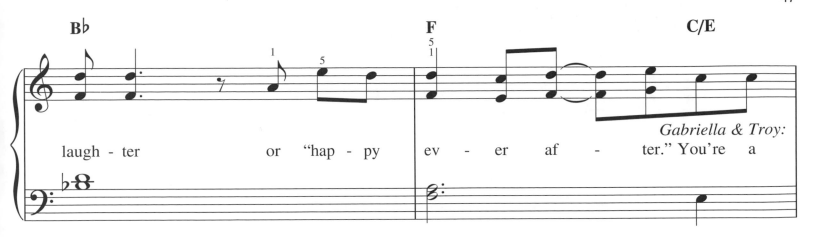

laugh - ter   or "hap - py   ev - er   af - ter." You're a

Gabriella & Troy:

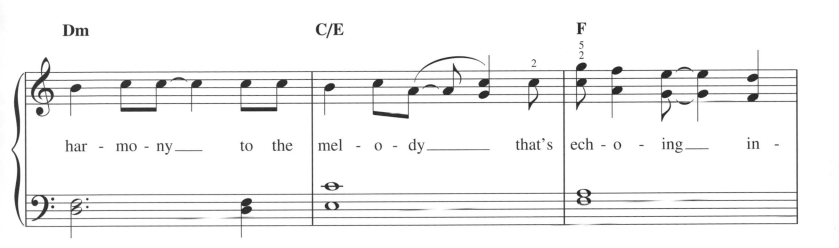

har - mo - ny____ to the   mel - o - dy____ that's ech - o - ing in -

side my   head.__ A   sin - gle voice_ a - bove the noise____ and

Gabriella:

G/T: like   a   com - mon thread,   *Troy:* mm,   you're pull - ing me.

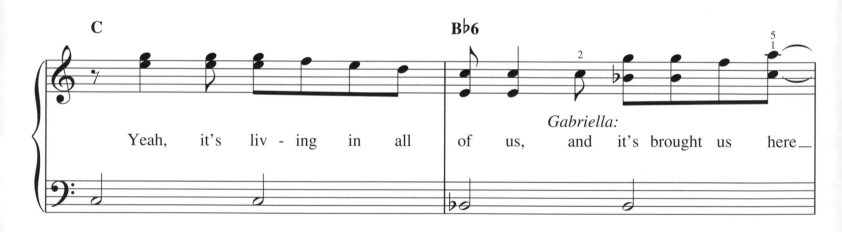

As I *Both:* am ____ you un - der - stand, ____ and

that's more than ____ I've ev - er known. _____ *Gabriella:* To

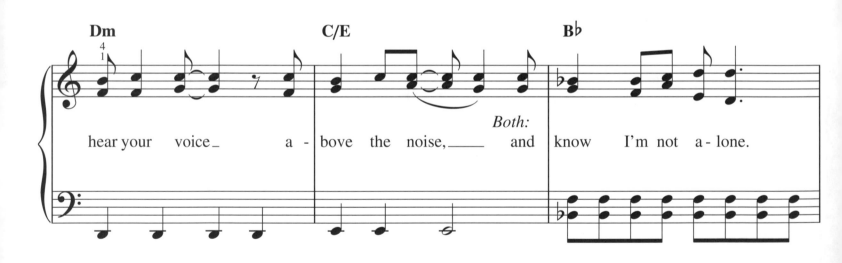

hear your voice _ a - bove the noise, ____ *Both:* and know I'm not a - lone.

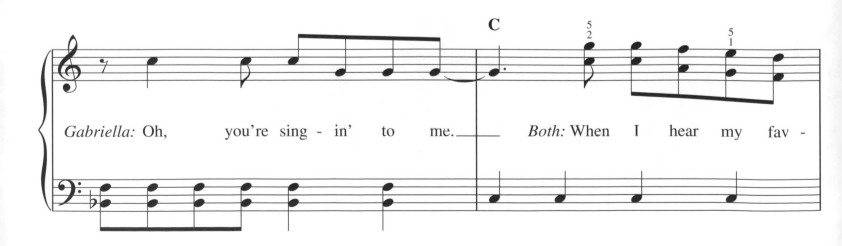

Gabriella: Oh, you're sing - in' to me. ____ *Both:* When I hear my fav -

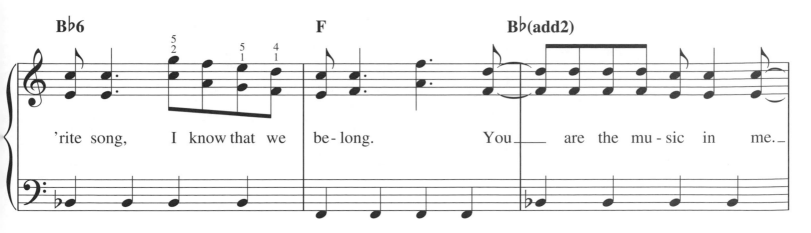

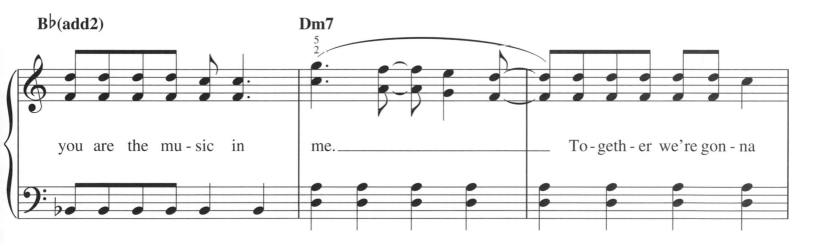

Gabriella:
nect-ed and real,__ can't keep it all__ in-side.

C   **B♭6**   **F**

All: (Na, na, na, na.)   (Na, na, na, na, na.)   (Na, na, na, na. You__

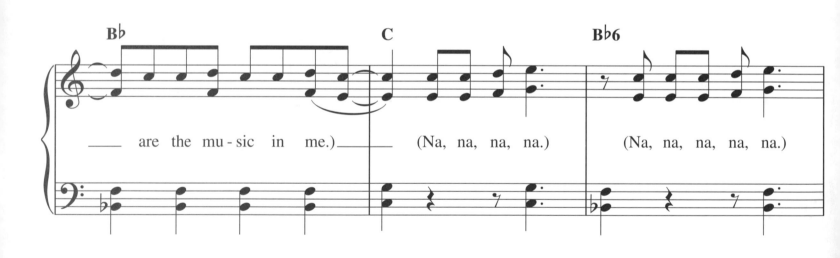

B♭   **C**   **B♭6**

__ are the mu-sic in me.)__   (Na, na, na, na.)   (Na, na, na, na, na.)

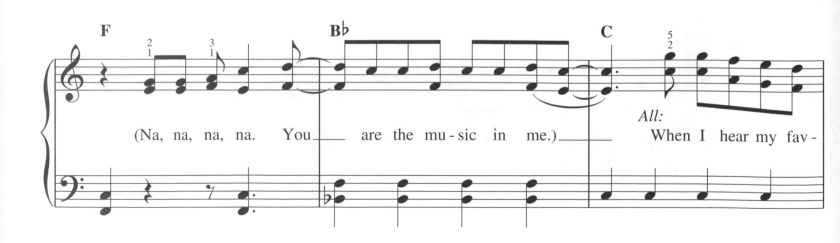

F   **B♭**   **C**

(Na, na, na, na. You__ are the mu-sic in me.)__   *All:*
When I hear my fav-

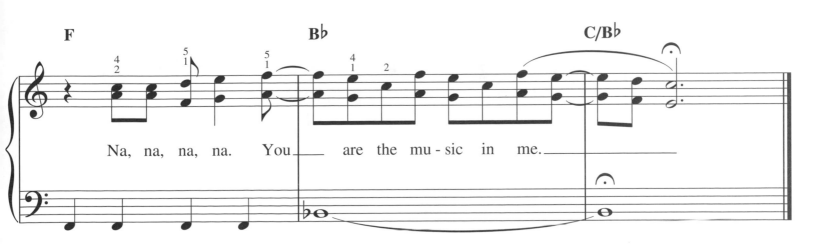

I DON'T DANCE

Words and Music by MATTHEW GERRARD
and ROBBIE NEVIL

Am

wan - na play ball now, and | that's all. This is what I | do. It ain't no
got what it takes, play - in' | my game, | so you bet - ter spin that

F

dance that you can | show me. | I'll show you
pitch you're gon - na | throw me, yeah. | I'll show you

Dm   **Em**   **F**

how I swing. } *Girls:* You'll nev - er know if

G

you nev - er try. *Chad:* There's just one lit - tle thing

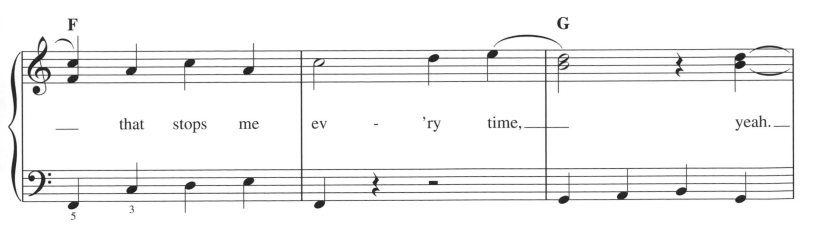

that stops me ev - 'ry time,____ yeah.____

____ *Ryan:* (Come on!)____ *Chad:* I don't dance. (I know you can.)_

Ryan/Girls:

____ *Chad:* Not a chance. *Ryan/Girls:* (If I could do this, well,

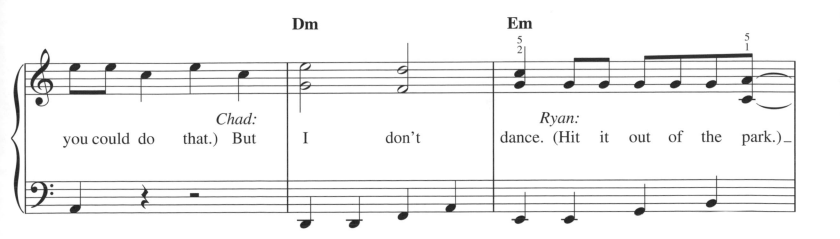

you could do that.) But I don't dance. (Hit it out of the park.)_

Chad:

Ryan:

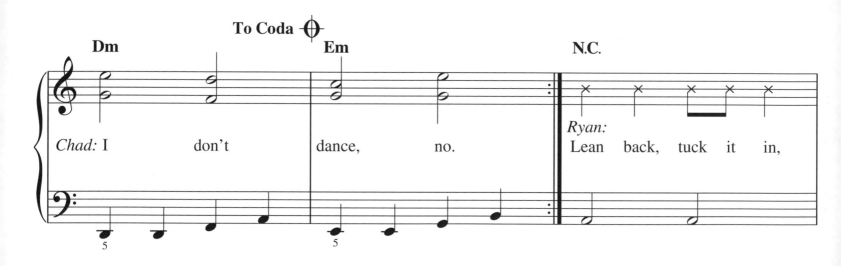

Chad: I wan-na play ball, not dance hall. I'm mak-in' a tri-ple, not a

cur-tain call.— *Ryan:* I can prove it to you 'til you know it's true,— 'cause I can

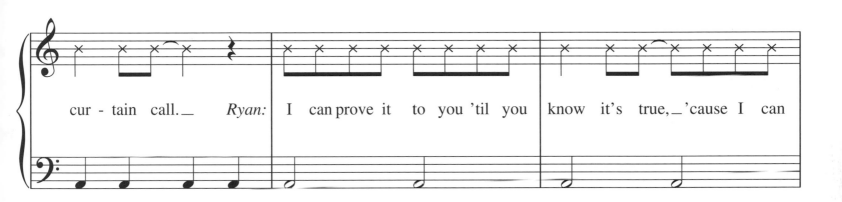

swing it, I can bring it to the dia-mond, too. *Chad:* You're talk-in' a lot;

show me what you got. Stop. *All:* Swing!—

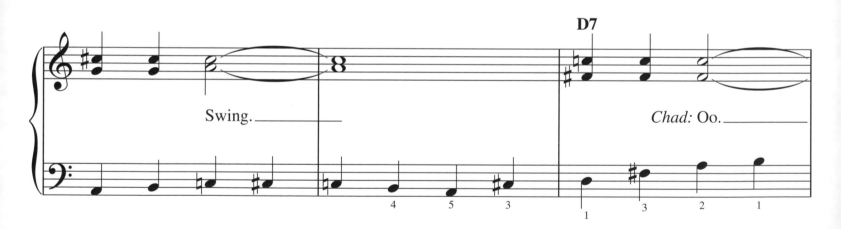

E

That's what I mean;   that's how you swing.   *Chad:* You make a good pitch but I

don't be - lieve.___   *Ryan:* I say you can.   *Chad:* I know I can't.

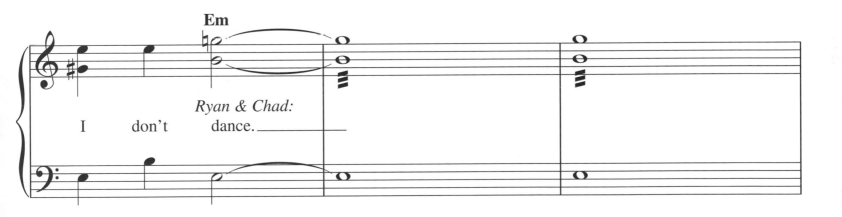

Em

Ryan & Chad: I don't dance._____

N.C.

At - ta boy, at - ta boy. Yeah. *Chad:* Hey, bat - ter, bat - ter, hey,

D.S. al Coda

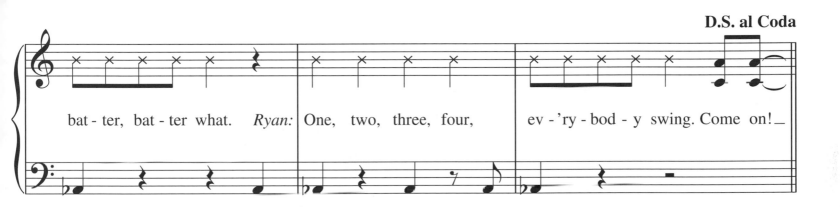

bat - ter, bat - ter what. *Ryan:* One, two, three, four, ev -'ry - bod - y swing. Come on!

CODA

Em   E7

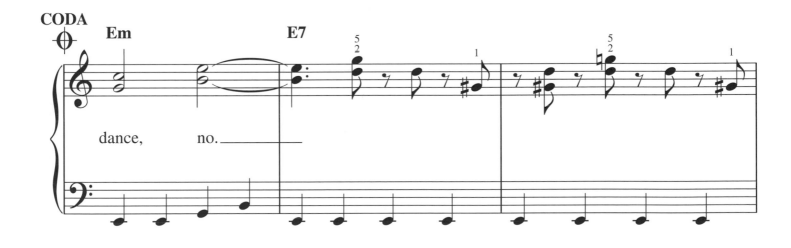

dance, no.

Am

GOTTA GO MY OWN WAY

Words and Music by ADAM WATTS
and ANDY DODD

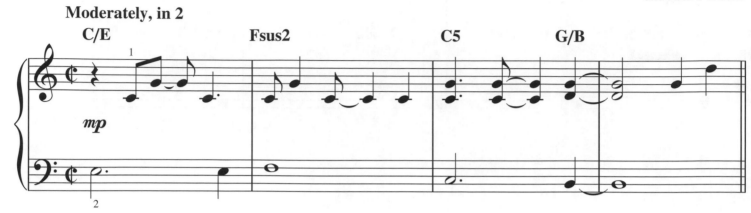

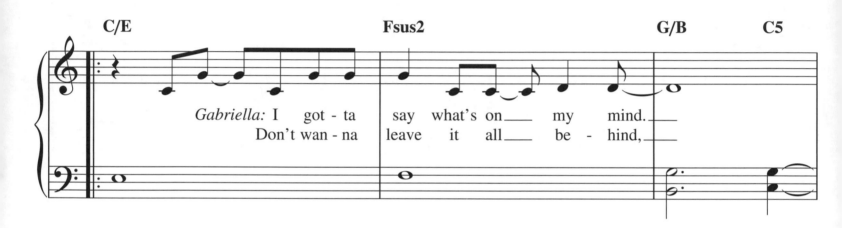

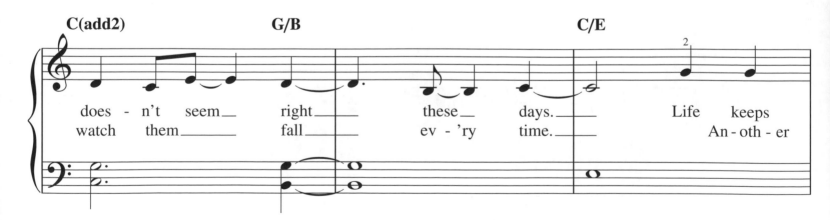

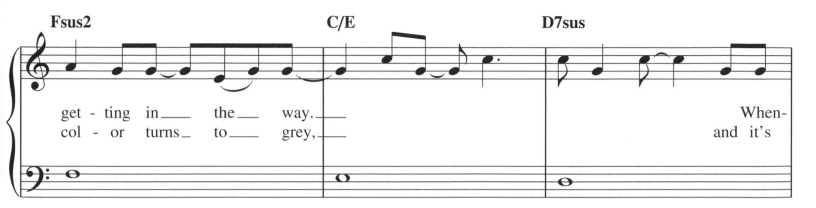

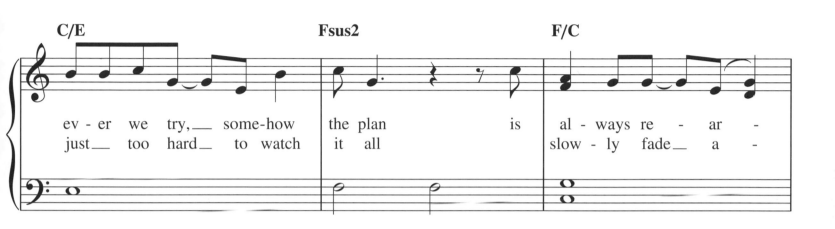

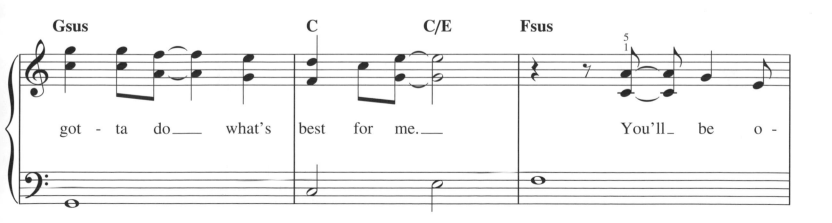

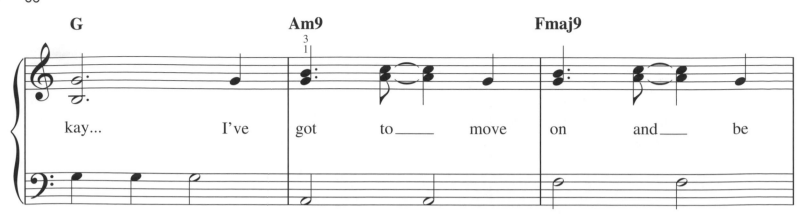

kay... I've got to__ move on and__ be

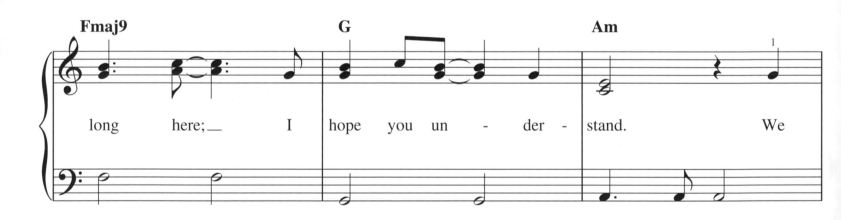

who I__ am.__ I just don't__ be -

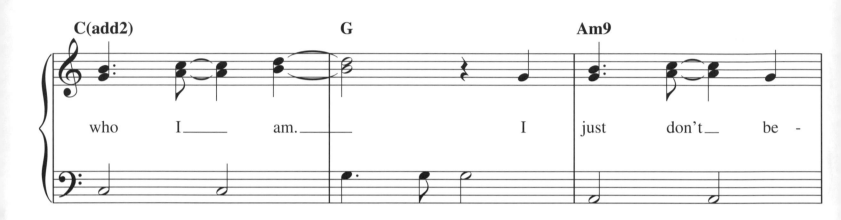

long here;__ I hope you un - der - stand. We

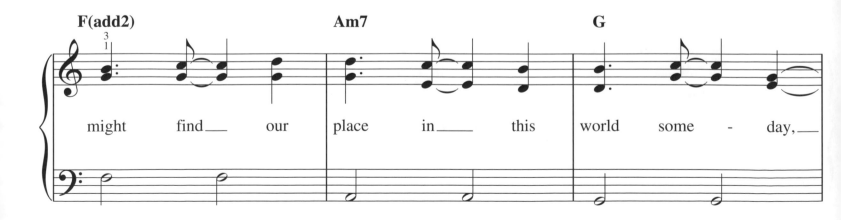

might find__ our place in__ this world some - day,__

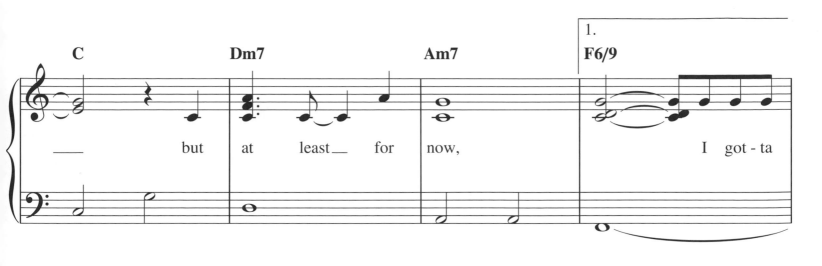

C   **Dm7**   **Am7**   **1.** **F6/9**

_____ but at least___ for now,   I got - ta

C/E   **Fsus2**

go my own_____ way._____

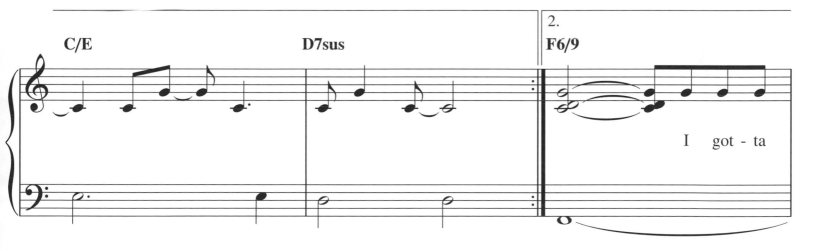

C/E   **D7sus**   **2.** **F6/9**

     I got - ta

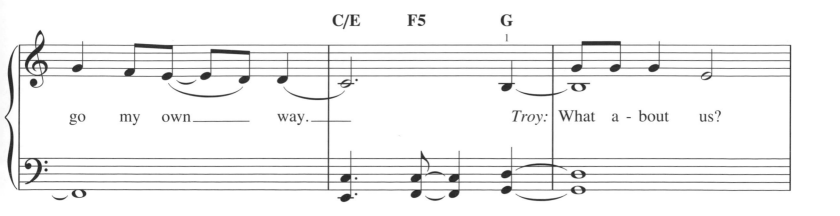

C/E   **F5**   **G**

go my own_____ way.___   _Troy:_ What a - bout us?

G/B   C5   Dm11   C/E   F5   G

What a - bout ev - 'ry - thing___ we've been through?___

C   Am11

Gabriella:
What a - bout trust?

Troy:
You know I nev - er want - ed to hurt___

C/E   F5   G   G/B   C5   Dm11

___ you.___

Gabriella:
And what a - bout me?___

Troy: What am

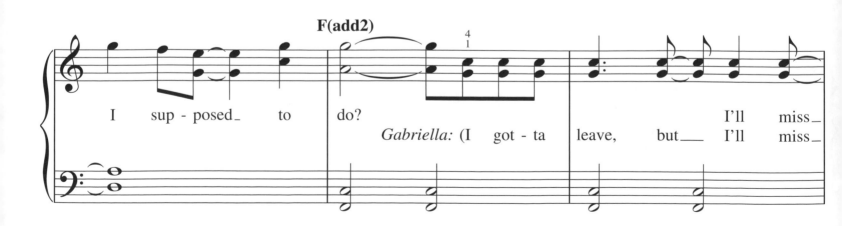

F(add2)

I sup - posed___ to do?

Gabriella: (I got - ta leave, but___ I'll miss___

I'll miss___

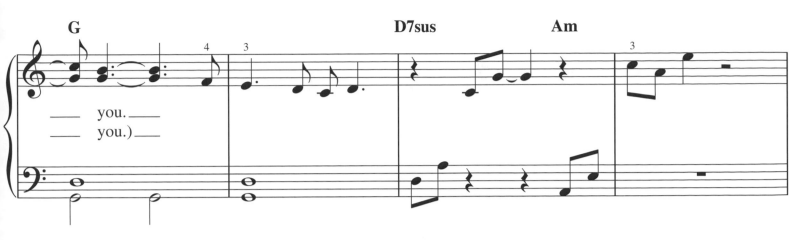

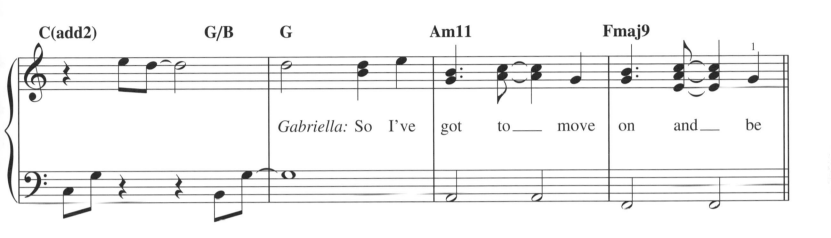

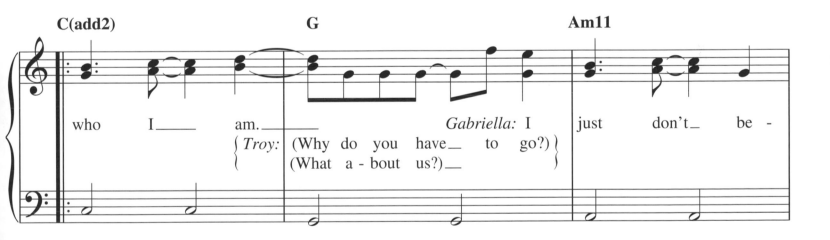

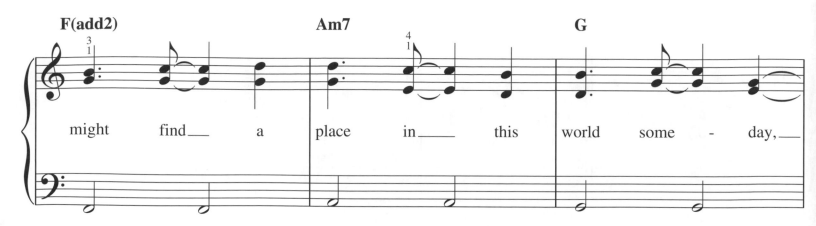

might find___ a place in___ this world some - day,___

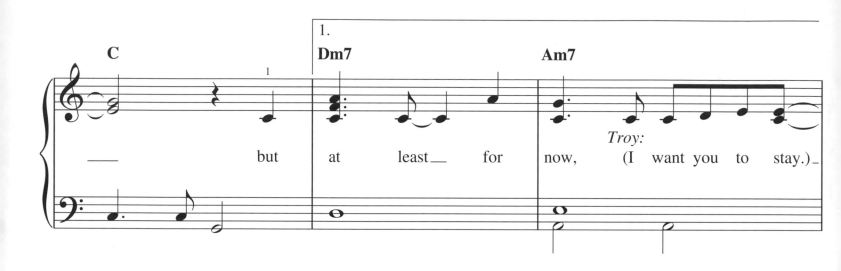

___ but at least___ for now, (I want you to stay.)___

Troy:

___ *Gabriella:* I wan - na go my own___ way. *Gabriella:* I've got to___ move

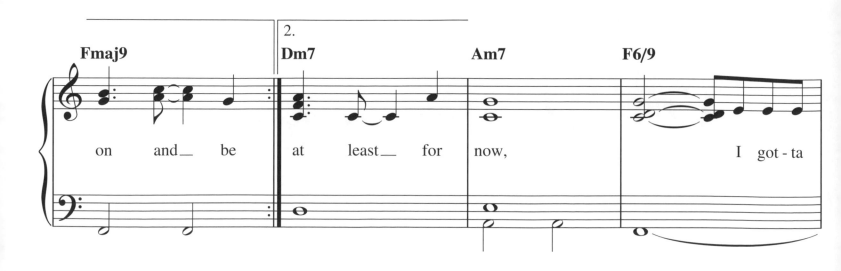

on and___ be at least___ for now, I got - ta

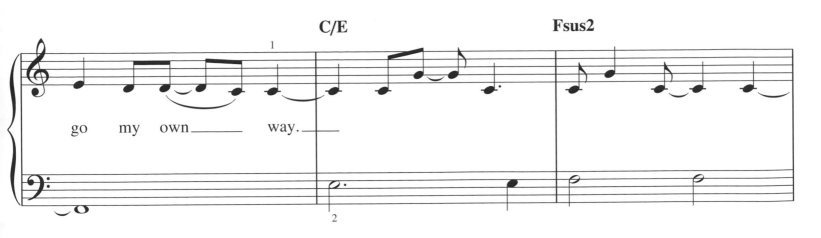

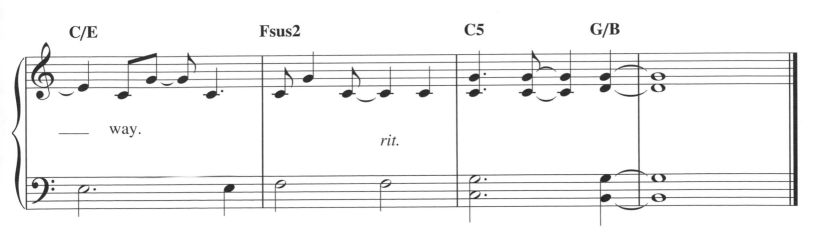

ALL FOR ONE

Words and Music by MATTHEW GERRARD
and ROBBIE NEVIL

Moderately fast

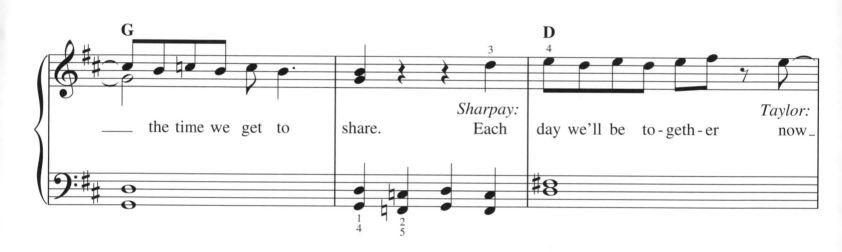

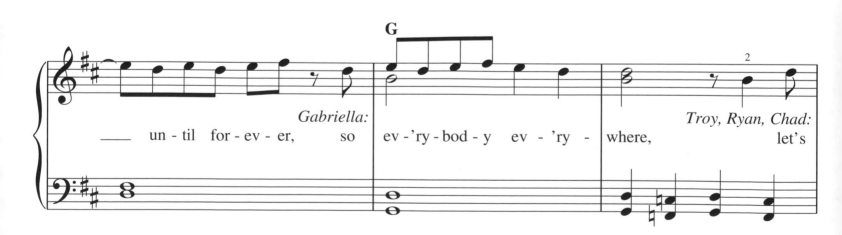

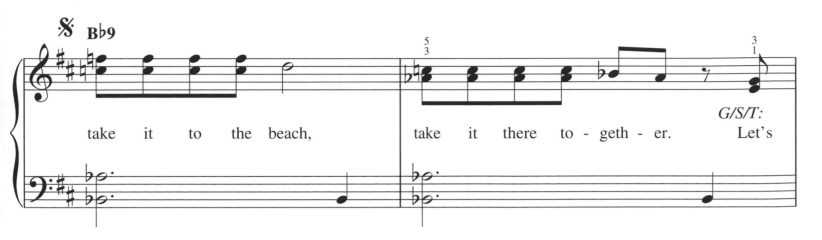

take it to the beach, take it there to - geth - er. *G/S/T:* Let's

cel - e - brate to - day, 'cause there'll nev - er be an - oth - er. *T/R/C:* We're

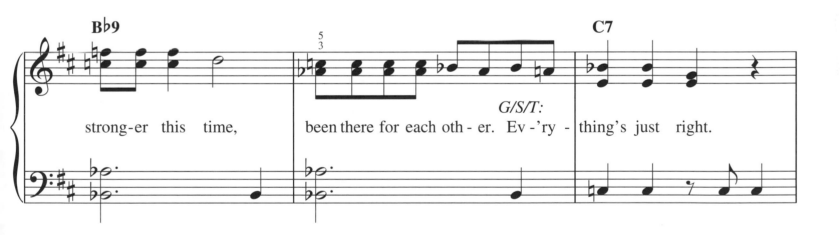

strong - er this time, been there for each oth - er. *G/S/T:* Ev - 'ry - thing's just right.

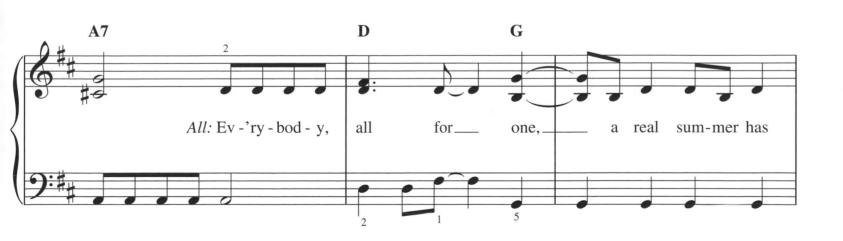

All: Ev -'ry - bod - y, all for____ one,____ a real sum - mer has

74

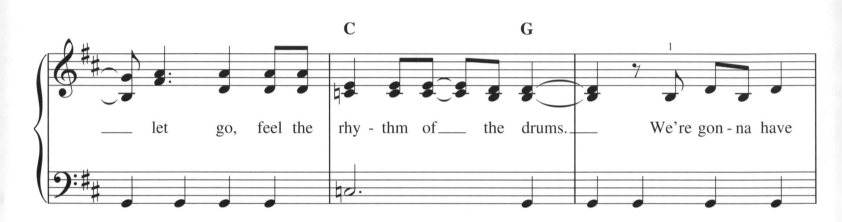

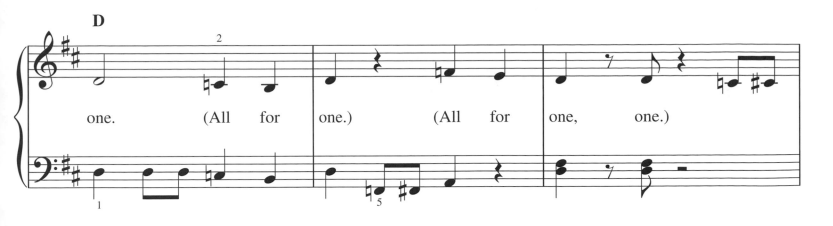

D

one.   (All   for   one.)   (All   for   one,   one.)

Sharpay: Sum-mer-time to-geth-er,   now___ *Taylor:* we're e - ven clos-er.

G   **D7**

Gabriella:
That's the way it's meant to be.___   *Chad:* Oh,   we're just get-ting start-ed.

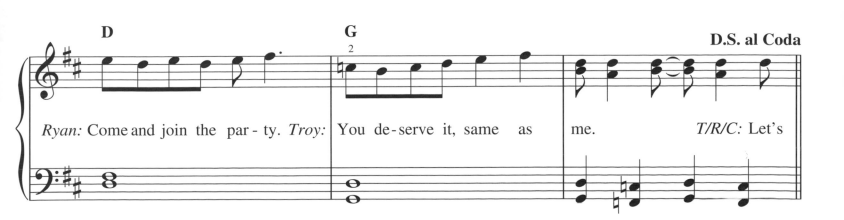

D   **G**   **D.S. al Coda**

Ryan: Come and join the par - ty. *Troy:* You de-serve it, same   as   me.   *T/R/C:* Let's

CODA

one.

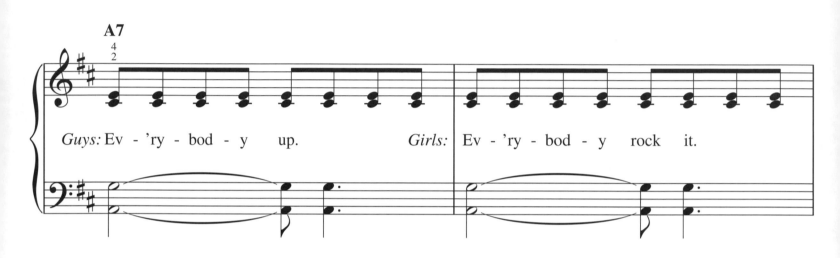

Guys: Ev - 'ry - bod - y up.   *Girls:* Ev - 'ry - bod - y rock it.

Guys: Take it from the top   *Girls:* and   nev - er, ev - er stop it.   *Guys:* It's

not a - bout the fu - ture, *Girls:* it's   not a - bout the past.   *All:* It's

mak - in' ev -'ry sin - gle day last and last___ and last. *All:* Fun and sun...

what could be bet - ter?

Let's have fun, ev -'ry - one to - geth - er now.___ (Ev -'ry - bod - y, e -

- ev -'ry - bod - y now.) This is where our sum - mer real - ly be -

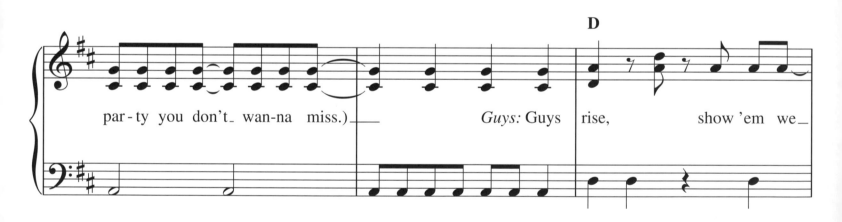

know how to groove, oh. *Guys:* Here *Girls:* and now, *Guys:* let's turn the par-ty *Girls:* out.

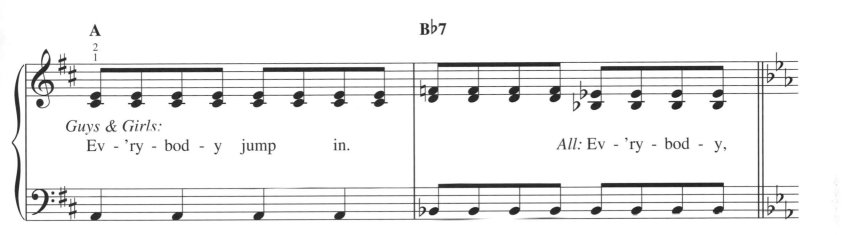

A **B♭7**

Guys & Girls: Ev-'ry-bod-y jump in. *All:* Ev-'ry-bod-y,

E♭ **A♭** **D♭** **A♭**

all for one, a real sum-mer has just be-gun.

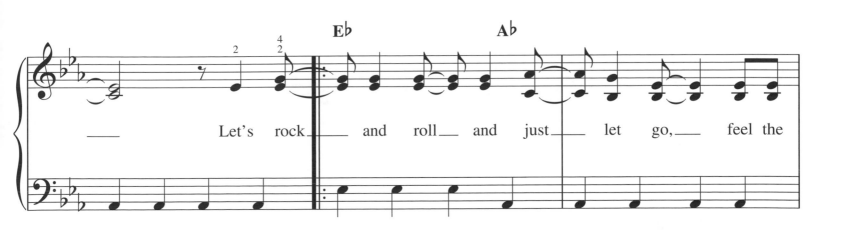

E♭ **A♭**

Let's rock and roll and just let go, feel the

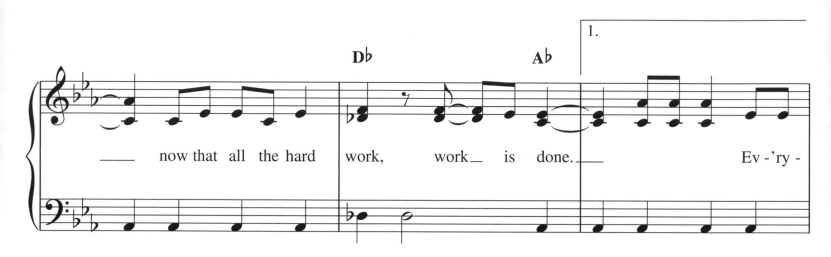

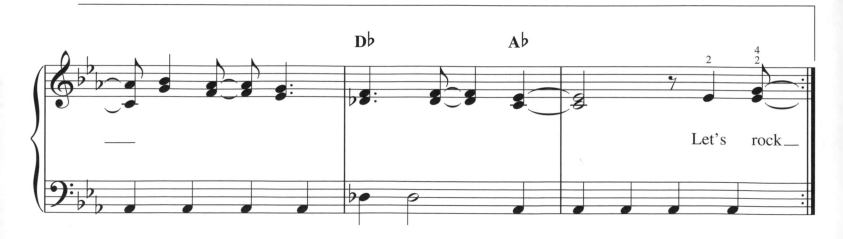

HUMU HUMU NUKU NUKU APUAA

Words and Music by DAVID LAWRENCE
and FAYE GREENBERG

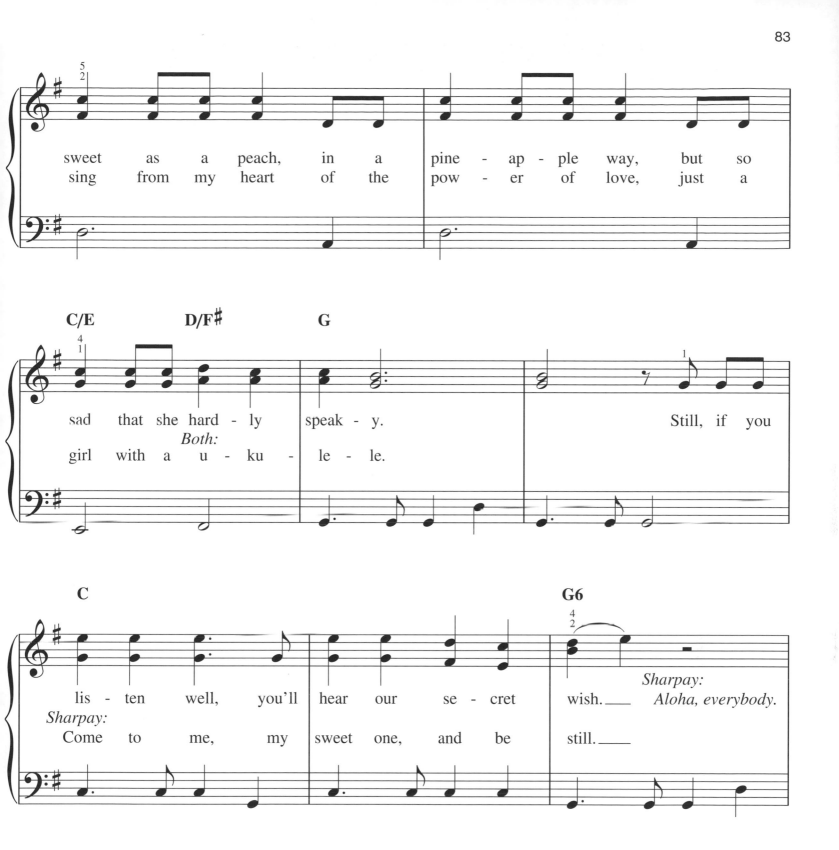

sweet as a peach, in a pine - ap - ple way, but so
sing from my heart of the pow - er of love, just a

C/E   **D/F#**   **G**

sad that she hard - ly speak - y.   Still, if you
Both:
girl with a u - ku - le - le.

C   **G6**

lis - ten well, you'll hear our se - cret wish.___ *Aloha, everybody.*
Sharpay:
Come to me, my sweet one, and be still.___

A

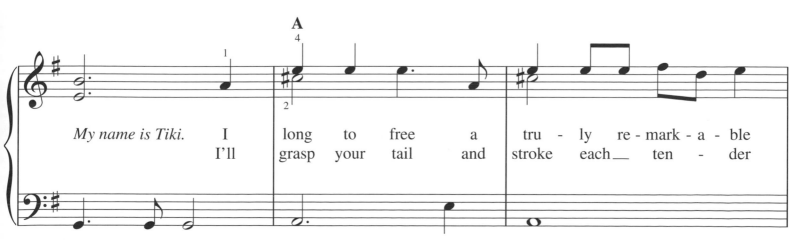

My name is Tiki. I long to free a tru - ly re - mark - a - ble
I'll grasp your free tail and stroke each___ ten - der

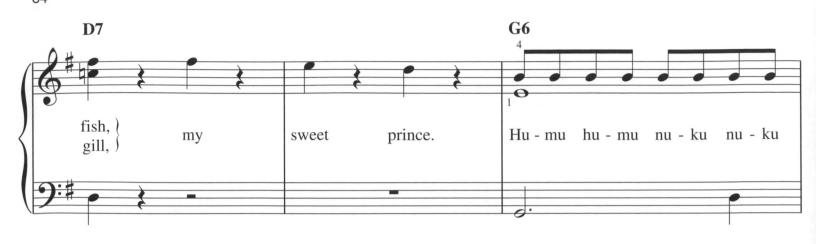

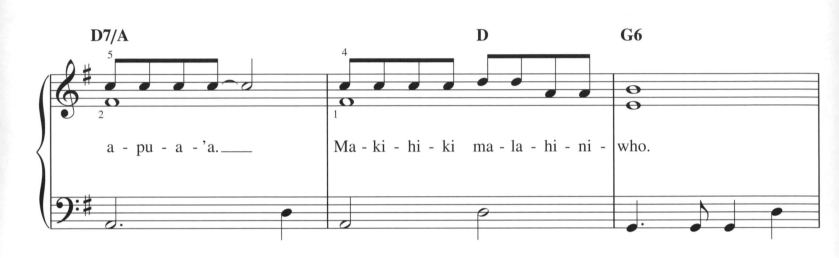

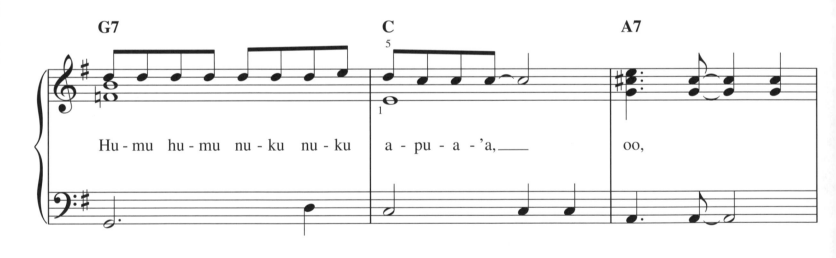

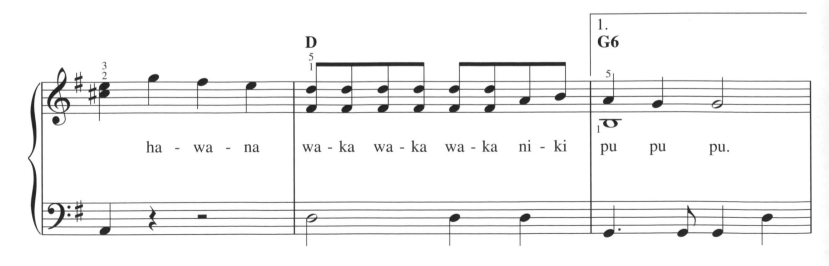

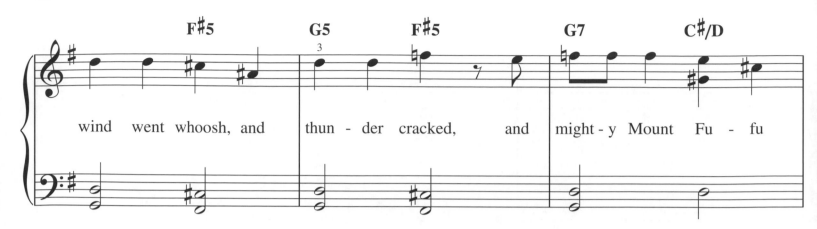

F#5   G5   F#5   G7   C#/D

wind went whoosh, and   thun - der cracked,   and   might - y Mount Fu - fu

G5   C#/D   G5

spit.   *Sharpay:* Might - y Mount Fu - fu   spit! *Ryan/Sharpay:* T - T - T -

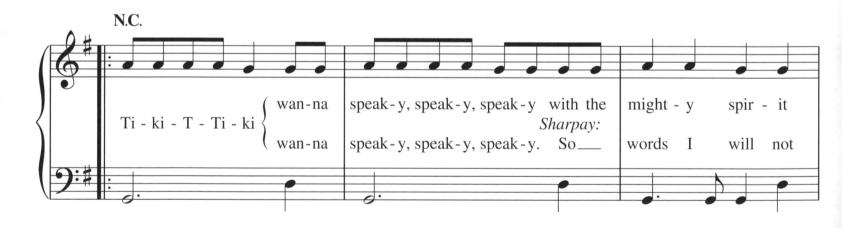

N.C.

Ti - ki - T - Ti - ki { wan-na   speak-y, speak-y, speak-y with the   might - y   spir - it
Sharpay:
wan-na   speak-y, speak-y, speak-y. So___ words I will not

1.   2.

Fu - fu.   T - T - T - mince.   Please make a man___ of my

fresh   fish   prince.

This is real fish talk... No lie.

(Vocal sound effects and gurgling)

Sharpay: And then the fish

turns into a gorgeous prince and sings, "I'm Prince

G

Hu - mu hu - mu nu - ku nu - ku

D7/A

a - pu - a - 'a,____   a -

D7

ma - ka - hi - ki ma - la - hi - ni -

G

who."   *With me!*

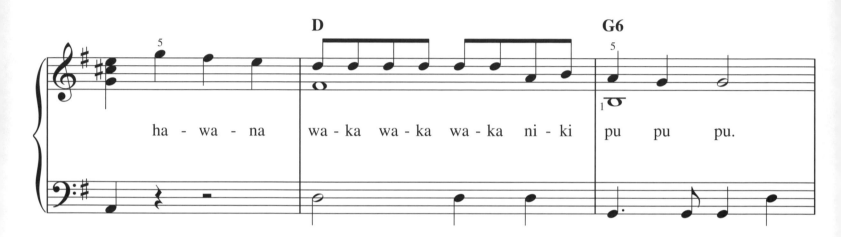

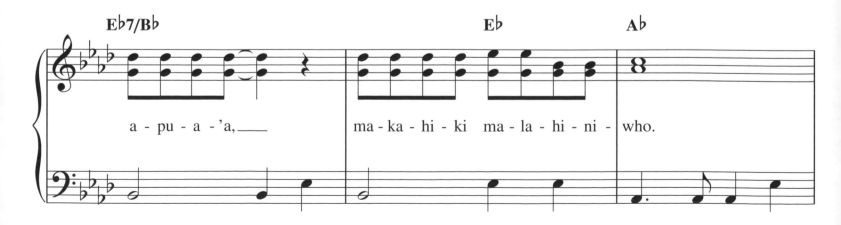

BET ON IT

Words and Music by TIM JAMES
and ANTONINA ARMATO

91

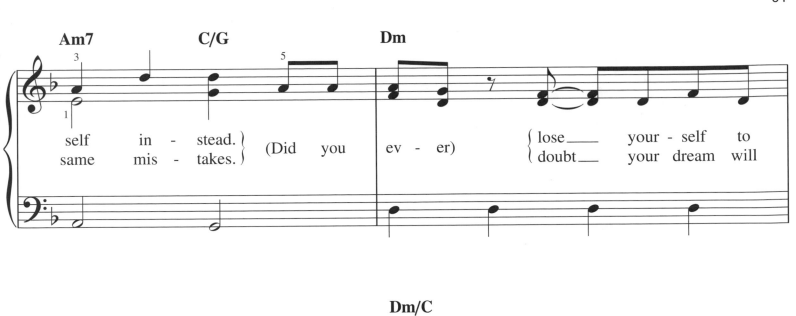

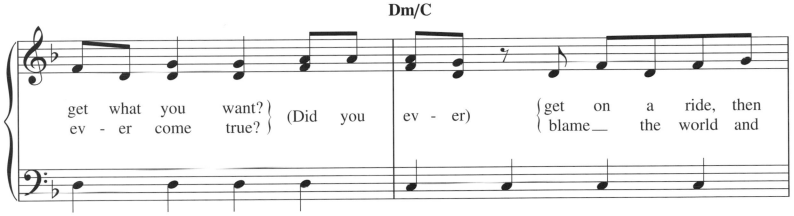

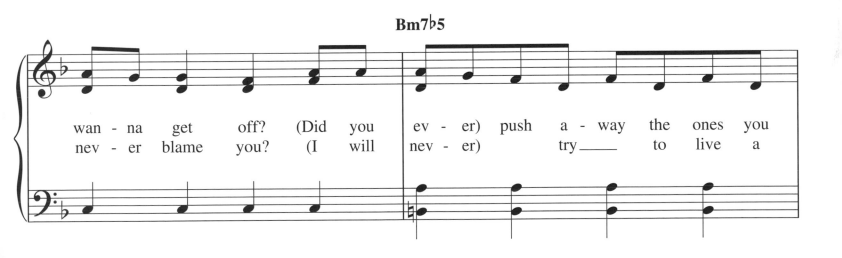

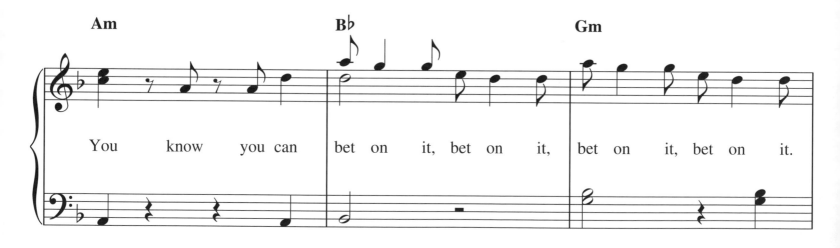

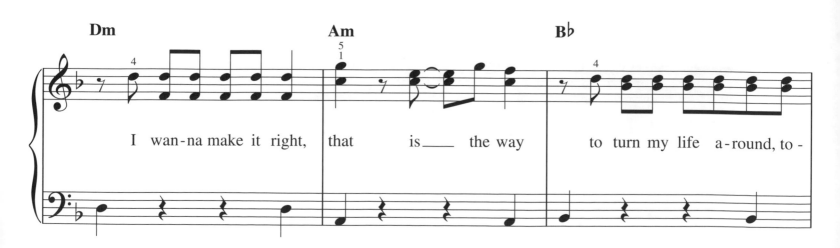

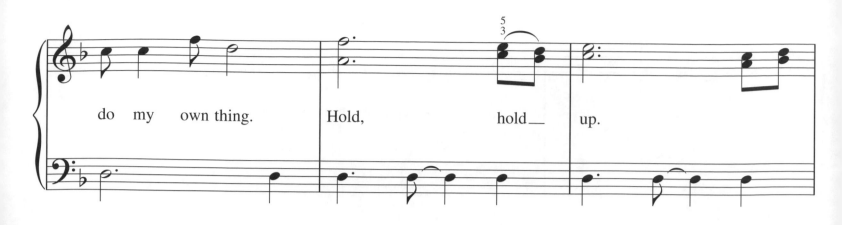

do my own thing. Hold, hold up.

Bbmaj7

It's no good at

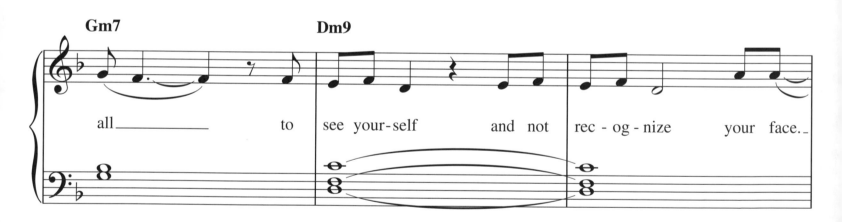

Gm7   Dm9

all_____ to see your-self and not rec-og-nize your face._

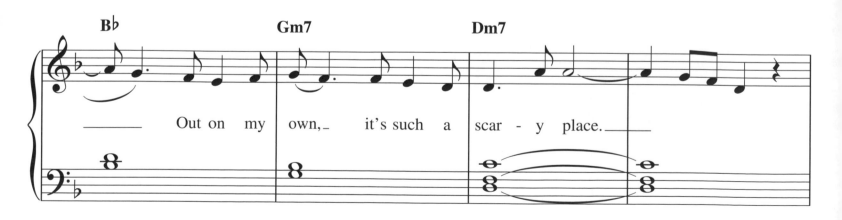

Bb   Gm7   Dm7

_____ Out on my own,_ it's such a scar-y place._

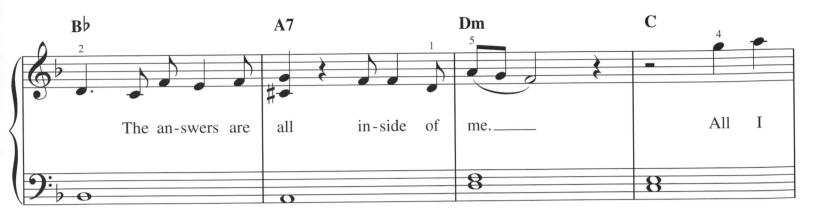

The an-swers are all in-side of me._____ All I

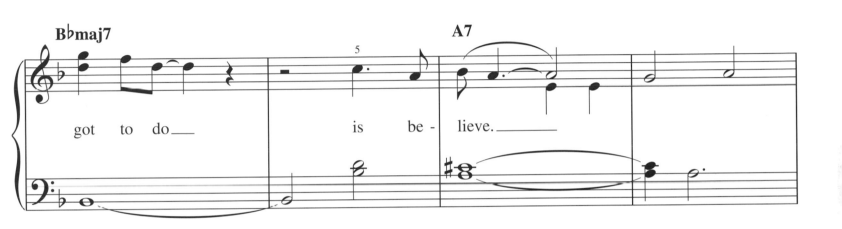

got to do___ is be - lieve._____

I'm not gon - na stop, not gon-na stop till I get my shot.

That's who I am, that is my plan. We'll end up on top. You can bet on it, bet on it,

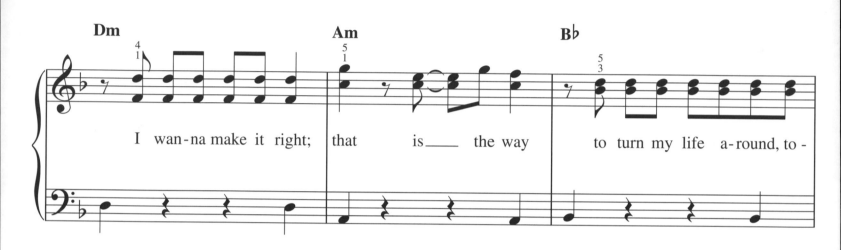

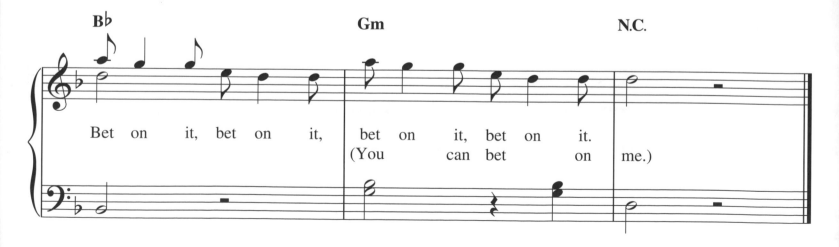